Test Equipment Management

201
Q&A

SAP Certified Application Associate
PLM-QM

ALSO BY BILLIE G. NORDMEYER

Test Equipment Management

201
Q&A

SAP Certified Application Associate
PLM-QM

Billie G. Nordmeyer, MBA, MA

Copyright © 2014 by Billie G. Nordmeyer
First Edition, 2014

Library of Congress Cataloging in Publication Data has been applied for.

ISBN 13: 978-1503120983
ISBN 10: 1503120988

ABOUT THE AUTHOR

Billie G. Nordmeyer, MBA, MA is an SAP consultant, trainer and published author. She has held Senior Consultant and Business Development Manager of SAP Practice positions with a "Big 4" consulting firm, three Fortune 100 firms and six Fortune Most Admired Companies. Nordmeyer has consulted with Fortune 100 and Fortune 500 enterprises and supported clients in the aerospace, oil and gas, software, retail, pharmaceutical and manufacturing industries. Nordmeyer holds a BSBA in accounting, an MBA in finance and an MA in international management.

CONTENTS

INTRODUCTION

A technical certification is a valuable achievement in part because employers consider it confirmation that a job candidate is a well-qualified professional. Accordingly, if your goal is a position with a consulting firm, a major firm in industry or a leading not-for-profit organization, SAP certification training will help you get there. SAP training aimed at enhancing your understanding of particular concepts so you might sit for a standardized exam and obtain a professional credential is available both online and at bricks-and mortar institutions. But some training programs fail to accomplish the key objective...namely, prepare a candidate to achieve a passing grade on a certification exam.

In an exam setting, you must identify correct answers to questions that may bear little resemblance to the way major concepts are presented in the day-to-day operation of SAP applications. Consequently, while in your professional life you may play a key role in support of SAP software and solutions, to do well on the exam, you'll need training that provides a global view of interrelated functions and activities. But some training programs fail to provide a certification candidate either the information needed to perform well during a testing process or the means necessary to identify his training needs.

You should also be aware that SAP certification exams assume that, as a certification candidate, you're knowledgeable about definitions and master data, as well as the application of a fairly extensive set of transactions and customizing functions. For example, during the testing process, you may be expected to recognize specific attributes of major transactions and customizing functions, definitions of key system elements, the interrelationship among all of these factors, or other characteristics of the system to which you may not be exposed on a daily basis. Your training program, however, may fail to provide a sufficient number of questions and explanations for you to learn or confirm your knowledge of even the most perfunctory concepts addressed by the certification exam.

What's more, when sitting for the certification exam and the answer to each question is one of several different -- and often complex -- alternatives, you want to be assured ahead of time that you can make the right choice. Reviewing documentation or working through a relatively small number of practice test questions, however, may not provide you with the practical skills needed to apply your knowledge in a multiple-choice testing environment.

Hence this book series for the SAP Certified Application Consultant PLM-QM exam that allows you to enhance and test your knowledge using hundreds of multiple-choice questions well before you take the actual exam. The 201 Q&A SAP Certified Application Consultant PLM-QM book series is composed of individual books, each of which addresses one module, scenario or master data that may be covered in the certification exam. In turn, each study guide, such as Calibration Inspections, provides both a short and detailed answer for each of the 201 questions included in the book. These explanations allow you to grasp the bigger picture, connect new information with prior knowledge and use this knowledge to increase your score on the actual exam.

In the case that you want to review and analyze your knowledge pertaining to only one topic, you can purchase the one book that addresses that topic. If instead, you want to review a number of topics the exam may address, you can purchase some or all of the books in the series. In either case, using the 201 practice exam questions provided in each book, you can analyze your training needs in regards to one function, scenario or master data and then focus your study on the specific areas where you need to enhance your knowledge. In either case, I wish you the best of luck on the exam!

CHAPTER I

QUESTIONS

QUESTIONS

Q-1:   Which of the following describes a primary function of the Test Equipment Management component? Select all that apply.

A. Inspect and calibrate test equipment used to perform quality inspections

B. Manage the inspection and maintenance of test equipment using equipment master records

C. Process the plant maintenance order

D. Schedule calibration inspections per maintenance orders and maintenance strategies

E. Manage the status of the maintenance plan, maintenance schedule and maintenance order

Short Answer: 93
Answer & Explanation: 113

Q-2:   Which of the following is an action that's triggered by a calibration inspection usage decision? Select all that apply.

A. Update status in equipment master record

B. Create maintenance order

C. Update cycle modification factor

D. Create notification item

Short Answer: 93
Answer & Explanation: 114

Q-3: Which of the following is a step in the Inspection Lot Creation phase of a calibration inspection?

A. Create equipment master record

B. Create inspection lot

C. Create master inspection characteristic

D. Schedule maintenance strategy

Short Answer: 93
Answer & Explanation: 114

Q-4: The time-based maintenance cycle that determines the calibration inspection dates and inspection scope is defined using which of the following?

A. Maintenance task list

B. Maintenance plan

C. Maintenance strategy

Short Answer: 93
Answer & Explanation: 115

Q-5: Identify a valid maintenance task list type that's used to maintain test equipment. Select all that apply.

A. Equipment task list

14

B. Routing

C. General maintenance task list

D. Functional location task list

E. Master recipe

Short Answer: 93
Answer & Explanation: 116

Q-6:   What would you use to monitor the status of
test equipment maintenance tasks?

A. Equipment master record

B. Measurement document

C. Maintenance order

Short Answer: 93
Answer & Explanation: 117

Q-7:   The system does not allow the entry of
qualitative measurement results for a measuring point
for test equipment. What could be the issue?

A. Test equipment status was not recorded as
    measurement point was created

B. Measurement point type was not recorded as
    measurement point was created

C. Qualitative characteristic with selected set was not
    assigned to the measurement point

Short Answer: 93
Answer & Explanation: 118

Q-8:   You want to update measurement documents automatically for an inspection lot during a calibration inspection. How does the system determine the characteristic data to be recorded?

A. Class characteristic with appropriate unit of measure is assigned to measuring point

B. Master inspection characteristic is created with reference to a class characteristic

C. Class characteristic is assigned to measuring point and master inspection characteristic

Short Answer: 93
Answer & Explanation: 118

Q-9:   What is the purpose of a maintenance item in a maintenance plan? Select all that apply.

A. Define maintenance object

B. Define maintenance schedule

C. Define maintenance task list

Short Answer: 93
Answer & Explanation: 119

Q-10:   What purpose does an equipment master record serve in Test Equipment Management? Select all that apply.

A. Provides the means to manage test equipment at the client level

B. Defines quantitative inspection specifications

C. Provides the means to document the maintenance history of test equipment

D. All of the above

E. None of the above

Short Answer: 94
Answer & Explanation: 120

Q-11: To plan maintenance and inspection tasks on a performance basis, what is required?

A. Single-cycle plan

B. Performance-based maintenance plan without maintenance strategy

C. Multiple-counter plan

D. All of the above

E. None of the above

Short Answer: 94
Answer & Explanation: 120

Q-12: The release of a maintenance order can automatically lead to which of the following?

A. Creation of inspection lot

B. Scheduling of maintenance strategy plan

C. Creation of equipment master record

Short Answer: 94
Answer & Explanation: 122

Q-13: What would you use to plan an inspection of test equipment on a one-time basis?

A. Single-cycle plan

B. Multiple-counter plan

C. Time-based maintenance plan

D. Performance-based maintenance plan

Short Answer: 94
Answer & Explanation: 123

Q-14: What is unique about the general maintenance task list?

A. The general maintenance task list is not linked to a maintenance object

B. The general maintenance task list serves as a proposal during the creation of maintenance order or maintenance task list

C. Master inspection characteristics are assigned to operations and sub-operations

D. Materials and resources required for maintenance work are planned for characteristic

Short Answer: 94
Answer & Explanation: 124

Q-15: What would you use to settle the costs incurred due to the performance of maintenance tasks?

A. Maintenance task list

B. Maintenance plan

C. Maintenance order

Short Answer: 94
Answer & Explanation: 125

Q-16:   What is a performance-based maintenance plan?

A. Point at which inspection tasks are performed is determined by counter readings

B. Point at which inspection tasks are performed is determined by defects recorded during prior inspection

C. Point at which inspection tasks are performed is determined by availability of inspectors and PRT

Short Answer: 94
Answer & Explanation: 126

Q-17:   What step in the calibration inspection planning process creates maintenance call dates on the basis of maintenance packages and scheduling parameters?

A. Create measuring point with reference to class characteristic

B. Update equipment status in equipment master record

C. Schedule maintenance plan

Short Answer: 94
Answer & Explanation: 126

Q-18: What components must be implemented to schedule and process calibration inspections? Select all that apply.

A. Plant Maintenance - Maintenance Processing

B. Plant Maintenance - Preventive Maintenance

C. Quality Management - Technical Objects

D. Plant Maintenance - Quality Planning

E. Quality Management – Inspections

Short Answer: 94
Answer & Explanation: 127

Q-19: Which of the following components is used to categorize test equipment based on its technical specifications?

A. Plant Maintenance – Technical Objects

B. Classification System

C. Quality Management – Quality Planning

Short Answer: 94
Answer & Explanation: 128

Q-20: The creation and release of the maintenance order, which triggers the inspection of test equipment, is performed by which of the following components?

A. Plant Maintenance

B. Test Equipment Management

C. Quality Management

D. Controlling

Short Answer: 94
Answer & Explanation: 128

Q-21:   A characteristic that is defined for a
calibration inspection is valuated on the wrong basis.
How is this error corrected?

A. Change valuation mode

B. Change sampling procedure

C. Change characteristic category

Short Answer: 95
Answer & Explanation: 129

Q-22:   Which of the following is a valid type of
maintenance plan that's created for test equipment?
Select all that apply.

A. Time-based maintenance plan with maintenance
   strategy

B. Performance-based maintenance plan with
   maintenance strategy

C. Multiple-counter maintenance plan with
   maintenance strategy

D. Time-based single cycle maintenance plan

E. Performance-based single cycle maintenance plan

Short Answer: 95

Answer & Explanation: 130

Q-23:   Identify an element of a maintenance task list structure. Select all that apply.

A. Operation

B. Sub-operation

C. Characteristic

Short Answer: 95
Answer & Explanation: 131

Q-24:   You want to perform a calibration inspection. How does the system determine the order in which inspection activities are performed?

A. Maintenance order

B. Maintenance task list operation

C. Maintenance plan

Short Answer: 95
Answer & Explanation: 132

Q-25:   The system does not allow the entry of quantitative measurement results for a measuring point for test equipment. What is a possible issue related to same?

A. Master inspection characteristics not assigned to measuring points

B. Equipment inspection point category not defined

C. Characteristic with selected set not assigned to measuring point

Short Answer: 95
Answer & Explanation: 133

Q-26:   In what ways does planning for one calibration inspection differ from the planning for another? Select all that apply.

A. Measurement document

B. Equipment master record

D. Task list

E. Inspection lot

E. Maintenance order

Short Answer: 95
Answer & Explanation: 134

Q-27:   The maintenance intervals documented in an equipment master record are defined on what basis? Select all that apply.

A. Equipment usage

B. Time schedule

C. Measuring point

D. Equipment number

E. Maintenance plan category

Short Answer: 95

Answer & Explanation: 135

Q-28: Which of the following is required to enter quantitative measurement results for test equipment measuring points?

A. Measuring point categories

B. Assignment of characteristic with selected set to measuring point

C. Assignment of class characteristics with unit of measure to measuring points

D. Assignment of class characteristics to master inspection characteristics

Short Answer: 95
Answer & Explanation: 136

Q-29: Which of the following objects can be assigned to a maintenance plan? Select all that apply.

A. Equipment task list

B. General task list

C. Class characteristic

D. Measuring point/counter

Short Answer: 95
Answer & Explanation: 136

Q-30: The confirmation of services for a maintenance order can be performed using what component?

A. Plant Maintenance

B. Test Equipment Management

C. Quality Management

D. Controlling

Short Answer: 95
Answer & Explanation: 137

Q-31:   How do you enable the use of both time-based and performance-based maintenance cycles for test equipment?

A. Maintenance plan

B. Maintenance task list

C. Equipment master record

Short Answer: 95
Answer & Explanation: 138

Q-32:   The customer wants particular maintenance tasks to be performed on particular dates. What is required?

A. Maintenance plan

B. Maintenance task list

C. Equipment master record

Short Answer: 95
Answer & Explanation: 139

Q-33:   PM technical objects, QM quality inspections and Classification System are used with the _____component to plan and schedule inspections.

A. QM Test Equipment Management

B. PM Preventive Maintenance

C. QM Quality Planning

Short Answer: 95
Answer & Explanation: 141

Q-34:   The user wants to create a maintenance history for test equipment. What record enables this requirement to be met?

A. Material master record

B. Maintenance order

C. Equipment master record

Short Answer: 96
Answer & Explanation: 141

Q-35:   The ability to record inspection results for the measuring points of test equipment requires which of the following?

A. Linkage of the inspection characteristic to class characteristic in the classification system

B. Linkage of the master inspection characteristic to class characteristic in the classification system

C. A or B

D. A and B

E. Neither A nor B

Short Answer: 96
Answer & Explanation: 142

Q-36: Define maintenance strategy, create equipment master record and create maintenance plan are examples of what?

A. Activities of the planning phase of a calibration inspection

B. Activities of the inspection lot creation phase of a calibration inspection

C. Activities of the processing phase of a calibration inspection

Short Answer: 96
Answer & Explanation: 142

Q-37: Which of the following is used to plan and schedule calibration inspections?

A. Maintenance order

B. Maintenance strategy

C. Maintenance plan

Short Answer: 96
Answer & Explanation: 143

Q-38:   Identify a characteristic of a maintenance task list. Select all that apply.

A. May consist of operations and sub-operations

B. May be an equipment, functional location or general maintenance task list

C. Inspection characteristics are assigned to operations and sub-operations

D. The operation can be performed by internal or external partner

Short Answer: 96
Answer & Explanation: 144

Q-39:   Why is the creation of a maintenance order mandatory for a calibration inspection? Select all that apply.

A. Plan inspection characteristics

B. Plan maintenance work to be performed at a particular work center

C. Settle costs of test equipment maintenance

Short Answer: 96
Answer & Explanation: 145

Q-40:   The customer wants the inspection lot for a calibration inspection to be automatically created on the basis of maintenance cycles in the maintenance plan. How is this requirement met?

A. Creation and release of maintenance order

B. Creation and release of maintenance task list

C. Creation and release of maintenance plan

Short Answer: 96
Answer & Explanation: 146

Q-41: Which of the following is a Customizing setting that's required to plan a calibration inspection? Select all that apply.

A. Inspection type

B. Inspection lot origin

C. Order type

D. All of the above

E. None of the above

Short Answer: 96
Answer & Explanation: 147

Q-42: For what purpose are the master inspection characteristics linked to class characteristics in the classification system?

A. Record inspection results for measuring points using measurement documents

B. Record inspection results for inspection characteristics using measurement documents

C. Record inspection results for inspection sample using measurement documents

Short Answer: 96
Answer & Explanation: 148

Q-43: What is required at the application level to create an equipment master record for a piece of test equipment?

A. Define equipment category

B. Create measuring point/counter with the required characteristic for the test equipment

C. Define inspection points

D. Define measuring point categories

Short Answer: 96
Answer & Explanation: 149

Q-44: Which of the following is used to create measuring points and counters for test equipment? Select all that apply.

A. Test Equipment Management: Create Measuring Point for Equipment

B. Test Equipment Management: Edit Equipment Master Record

C. Plant Maintenance: Create Task List

Short Answer: 96
Answer & Explanation: 150

Q-45: The customer wants to plan a calibration inspection. What activities will enable them to do so? Select all that apply.

A. Create material master record for each piece of test equipment

B. Form test equipment groups according to the maintenance strategy

C. Link master inspection characteristics to class characteristics using the classification system

D. Define inspection specifications for both quantitative and qualitative characteristics

Short Answer: 97
Answer & Explanation: 150

Q-46:   Which of the following is a planning function that belongs to the Test Equipment Management component?

A. Create Maintenance Task List

B. Create Test Equipment Master Record

C. Update PMIS

Short Answer: 97
Answer & Explanation: 151

Q-47:   The customer wants to accept or reject each piece of test equipment in an inspection lot on the basis of recorded inspection results. What calibration inspection function is used to do so?

A. Usage Decision

B. Maintenance Order Completion

C. Inspection Lot Completion

D. Results Recording

Short Answer: 97
Answer & Explanation: 152

Q-48:   Which of the following is a method that can be used to create measuring points for test equipment?

A. Create measuring point for equipment

B. Edit equipment master record

C. Create task list

Short Answer: 97
Answer & Explanation: 153

Q-49:   Identify a task list that is used in Plant Maintenance and is linked to a particular maintenance object.

A. General maintenance task list

B. Equipment task list

C. Functional location task list

Short Answer: 97
Answer & Explanation: 154

Q-50:   How does a customer change the work center at which an inspection will be performed?
A. Maintenance order

B. Maintenance schedule

C. Maintenance task list

Short Answer: 97
Answer & Explanation: 155

Q-51:   What can be referenced in a maintenance order operation?

A. Resource

B. Inspection type

C. Master inspection characteristic

Short Answer: 97
Answer & Explanation: 156

Q-52:   How does the system differentiate one set of work steps required for a calibration inspection from another?

A. Material master record

B. Maintenance task list

C. Maintenance order

Short Answer: 97
Answer & Explanation: 157

Q-53:   Which of the following is required to create an equipment master record for test equipment?

A. Select the production resource tool indicator for the equipment category test and measurement equipment in Plant Maintenance

B. Enter equipment key

C. Enter test equipment category

Short Answer: 97
Answer & Explanation: 158

Q-54: Measurement documents can be updated automatically as a follow-up action for a calibration inspection. Which of the following is required to do so?

A. Class characteristic is assigned to the master inspection characteristic and measuring point/counter

B. Master inspection characteristics

C. Number is assigned to each measuring point

Short Answer: 97
Answer & Explanation: 158

Q-55: What is the result of the assignment of a task list to a maintenance plan?

A. Maintenance plan is scheduled

B. Inspection can be conducted

C. Maintenance schedule is updated

Short Answer: 98
Answer & Explanation: 159

Q-56: Which of the following can occur as a calibration inspection is planned? Select all that apply.

A. Create test equipment group

B. Document maintenance history in equipment master record

C. Define task list

D. Link master inspection characteristics to inspection characteristics in the classification system

E. Define maintenance strategy

Short Answer: 98
Answer & Explanation: 160

Q-57: What is used to plan a calibration inspection?

A. Assign inspection type to material type

B. Define inspection type

C. Define order type

D. All of the above

E. None of the above

Short Answer: 98
Answer & Explanation: 161

Q-58: What is a requirement to document quantitative measurement results for measuring points? Select all that apply.

A. Enter measuring point category

B. Assign class characteristic to measuring point

C. Assign qualitative characteristic with selected set to a measuring point

Short Answer: 98
Answer & Explanation: 162

Q-59: An equipment master record is created for a piece of test equipment. Which of the following components is used to do so?

A. Plant Maintenance

B. Test Equipment Management

C. Quality Planning

Short Answer: 98
Answer & Explanation: 162

Q-60: Which of the following can be updated with data generated by the Test Equipment Management component? Select all that apply.

A. Plant Maintenance Information System

B. Quality Management Information System

C. Financial Information System

Short Answer: 98
Answer & Explanation: 163

Q-61: How does the system determine the tasks to be performed during a calibration inspection?

A. Maintenance plan

B. Maintenance task list

C. Maintenance strategy

Short Answer: 98
Answer & Explanation: 163

Q-62: Which of the following describes a time-based maintenance plan?

A. Tasks of maintenance task list are scheduled on a calendar basis

B. Tasks of maintenance task list are scheduled on the basis of the time that has passed since the last inspection

C. Tasks of maintenance task list are performed on a ad hoc basis in response to rejected valuation of characteristics

D. Tasks of maintenance task list are performed in sequence as determined by time required per operation

Short Answer: 98
Answer & Explanation: 165

Q-63: Identify a Customizing requirement for a calibration inspection?

A. Inspection type

B. Inspection points

C. Master inspection characteristic

D. Maintenance plan

E. Equipment master record

Short Answer: 98
Answer & Explanation: 166

Q-64: What would you use to define activities to be performed at a work center during a calibration inspection?

A. Maintenance strategy

B. Maintenance task list

C. Maintenance order

Short Answer: 98
Answer & Explanation: 166

Q-65: Which of the following is an assignment that must be made to conduct a calibration inspection? Select all that apply.

A. Assignment of task list to maintenance plan

B. Assignment of inspection characteristics to operations

C. Assignment of material type to order type

Short Answer: 98
Answer & Explanation: 168

Q-66: Quantitative measurement results are recorded for a measuring point for test equipment. However, the results seem to be incorrect. Why?

A. Incorrect class characteristic unit of measure

B. Incorrect class characteristic assigned to measuring point

C. Incorrect measuring point category

Short Answer: 99

Answer & Explanation: 168

Q-67:   What functions must be completed for a measurement document in Plant Maintenance to be automatically updated as a follow-up action for a calibration inspection?

A. Inspection characteristic created

B. Measuring point assigned to equipment

C. Measuring point created with reference to class characteristic

Short Answer: 99
Answer & Explanation: 169

Q-68:   The Test Equipment Management component is integrated with what other SAP ECC components to perform a calibration inspection? Select all that apply.

A. Plant Maintenance - Preventive Maintenance

B. Plant Maintenance - Maintenance Processing

C. Quality Management - Technical Objects

D. Quality Management - Quality Inspections

E. Plant Maintenance - Quality Planning

Short Answer: 99
Answer & Explanation: 170

Q-69:   Identify a valid function of the Test Equipment Management component. Select all that apply.

A. Create equipment master record

B. Schedule maintenance plan

C. Plan inspections for QM orders

D. Create maintenance plan for maintenance strategy

E. Maintain the linkage of inspection characteristics in the classification system to master inspection characteristics

Short Answer: 99
Answer & Explanation: 170

Q-70: How does the structure of one maintenance plan differ from another? Select all that apply.

A. Maintenance plan may be defined with or without a maintenance strategy

B. Maintenance plan may be time- and/or performance-based

C. Maintenance objects are maintained in maintenance strategy maintenance item

D. Performance-based maintenance plan is based on age of equipment

Short Answer: 99
Answer & Explanation: 171

Q-71:   The maintenance cycles that determine the calibration intervals for test equipment can be defined using which of the following?

A. Maintenance task list

B. Maintenance plan

C. Master inspection characteristic

Short Answer: 99
Answer & Explanation: 172

Q-72:   Which of the following is defined at the application level during the planning of a calibration inspection? Select all that apply.

A. Inspection characteristic

B. Equipment master record

C. Task list

D. Maintenance plan

Short Answer: 99
Answer & Explanation: 173

Q-73:   What is a primary difference between a maintenance plan with a maintenance strategy and one without?

A. The maintenance strategy enables a time-based or performance based maintenance plan to be executed on a recurring basis

B. The maintenance strategy enables the definition of operations or sub-operations to be performed in parallel or simultaneously

C. The maintenance plan is not linked to a maintenance object and can be copied to create the maintenance strategy

Short Answer: 99

Answer & Explanation: 174

Q-74:   A calibration interval based on time or
performance is an example of what?

A. Maintenance cycle defined for a maintenance plan

B. Maintenance cycle defined for a maintenance
    strategy

C. Maintenance cycle defined for a maintenance object

Short Answer: 99
Answer & Explanation: 175

Q-75:   How would you define maintenance call dates
for a calibration inspection?

A. Assign task list to maintenance plan

B. Create time-based strategy plan

C. Schedule maintenance plan

Short Answer: 99
Answer & Explanation: 176

Q-76:   Which of the following is a calibration
inspection planning function that's performed using the
Test Equipment Management component? Select all
that apply.

A. Create task list

B. Create equipment master record

C. Create measuring points, counters and measurement documents

Short Answer: 100
Answer & Explanation: 177

Q-77:   Which of the following is a calibration inspection processing function? Select all that apply.

A. Record Results

B. Schedule Maintenance Plan

C. Create Equipment Master Record

Short Answer: 100
Answer & Explanation: 178

Q-78:   How does the system determine the sample size as well as the basis on which an inspection characteristic is accepted or rejected during a calibration inspection?

A. Sampling type

B. Valuation rule

C. Sampling procedure

Short Answer: 100
Answer & Explanation: 179

Q-79:   A characteristic is accepted on the wrong basis during a calibration inspection. What is a possible source of this error?

A. Valuation mode

B. Sampling procedure

C. Characteristic category

D. Sampling type

Short Answer: 100
Answer & Explanation: 179

Q-80:   Test equipment maintenance intervals can be controlled on what basis?

A. Performance

B. Measuring points

C. Functional location

Short Answer: 100
Answer & Explanation: 180

Q-81:   What influences the performance of maintenance or inspection tasks that are performed on a maintenance object?

A. Service order

B. Maintenance plan

C. Maintenance strategy

Short Answer: 100
Answer & Explanation: 181

Q-82:   What is the purpose of defining sub-operations for a maintenance task list?

A. Define the spare materials required to perform the maintenance work

B. Define the individual steps of a calibration inspection in greater detail than would be possible if an operation were used

C. Define the maintenance order

D. Define the work center that's responsible for the conduct of the work required by the task list

Short Answer: 100
Answer & Explanation: 182

Q-83:   The customer requires the ability to plan maintenance tasks, monitor the completion of the tasks as well as account for the costs incurred to perform the tasks. What will enable him to do so?

A. Maintenance task list

B. Maintenance plan

C. Maintenance order

Short Answer: 100
Answer & Explanation: 183

Q-84:   The assignment of an inspection type to a maintenance order type is required if:

A. Maintenance order is to be created automatically as a maintenance plan is released

B. Inspection lot is to be created automatically as a maintenance order is released

C. Maintenance order is created automatically when task list is assigned to maintenance plan

Short Answer: 100
Answer & Explanation: 184

Q-85: A calibration inspection is completed. However, measurement documents were not automatically updated. What could be the reason?

A. Master inspection characteristics used

B. Class characteristic is not assigned to measuring point/counter and master inspection characteristic

C. Master inspection characteristic not assigned to measuring point/counter

Short Answer: 100
Answer & Explanation: 185

Q-86: Where are the settings made that determine the maintenance tasks to be performed on a due date?

A. Maintenance plan

B. Maintenance task list

C. Maintenance strategy

Short Answer: 100
Answer & Explanation: 186

Q-87: You want to perform a calibration inspection. How does the system determine the individual activities to be performed at specific work centers?

A. Maintenance plan

B. Maintenance task list

C. Maintenance strategy

Short Answer: 100
Answer & Explanation: 187

Q-88:   What component is required to create the master records used for test equipment?

A. Plant Maintenance

B. Quality Management

C. Materials Management

D. Production Planning

Short Answer: 100
Answer & Explanation: 188

Q-89:   Identify a possible follow-up action that can be triggered with a usage decision for test equipment. Select all that apply.

A. Update equipment status

B. Create notification item

C. Update inspection lot size

D. Update measurement documents

Short Answer: 101
Answer & Explanation: 188

Q-90: You want to schedule the test equipment maintenance tasks on a time basis. How is this accomplished? Select all that apply.

A. Time-based multiple counter plan

B. Time-based maintenance plan with maintenance strategy

C. Single-cycle time-based maintenance plan

D. All of the above

E. None of the above

Short Answer: 101
Answer & Explanation: 189

Q-91: Which of the following is a valid assignment in a maintenance task list? Select all that apply.

A. Material assigned to maintenance task list operation

B. Material assigned to maintenance task list sub-operation

C. Master inspection characteristic assigned to operation

D. Inspection characteristic assigned to sub-operation

Short Answer: 101
Answer & Explanation: 190

Q-92: The conditions that determine the acceptance or rejection of an inspection lot are defined for which of the following?

A. Inspection lot

B. Inspection operation

C. Inspection characteristic

Short Answer: 101
Answer & Explanation: 191

Q-93: The customer wants to enter qualitative measurement results for a measurement point for test equipment. What assignment is required to do so?

A. Assign class characteristic with unit of measure to measuring point

B. Assign qualitative characteristic with a selected set to the measuring point

C. Assign quantitative characteristic with selected set to the measuring point

Short Answer: 101
Answer & Explanation: 192

Q-94: The maintenance history for test equipment is maintained where?

A. Equipment master record

B. Maintenance plan

C. Maintenance order

Short Answer: 101
Answer & Explanation: 192

Q-95:   An equipment master record is created for which of the following?

A. Test equipment

B. Functional location

C. Inspection point

Short Answer: 101
Answer & Explanation: 193

Q-96:   The customer wants to plan recurring calibration inspections on a time basis. What is used to do so?

A. Multiple-counter plan

B. Time-based maintenance plan with maintenance strategy

C. Single-cycle time-based maintenance plan

D. Performance-based maintenance plan with maintenance strategy

E. Single-cycle performance-based maintenance plan

Short Answer: 101
Answer & Explanation: 193

Q-97:   What object grants the user a means to document required maintenance tasks as well as define the work center at which the tasks will be performed?

A. Maintenance task list

B. Maintenance strategy

C. Maintenance order

Short Answer: 101
Answer & Explanation: 194

Q-98:   A calibration inspection was performed.
However, appraisal costs were not recorded for the
inspection. What could be the origin of this error?

A. Order was not created

B. Order was not released

C. Incorrect order type

D. Incorrect order category

E. Any of the above

F. None of the above

Short Answer: 101
Answer & Explanation: 196

Q-99:   In what sequence does the system select
operations to be performed in a maintenance task list?

A. Operations are performed in chronological order

B. An operation assigned to one work center takes
   precedence over an operation assigned to many

C. All sub-operations are performed before operations

Short Answer: 101
Answer & Explanation: 196

Q-100:   A master inspection characteristic can be assigned to which of the following?

A. Operation in maintenance task list

B. Sub-operation in maintenance task list

C. Work center

Short Answer: 101
Answer & Explanation: 197

Q-101:   Create maintenance plan, create measurement points and define maintenance strategy are activities of what phase of a calibration inspection?

A. Planning

B. Inspection Lot Creation

C. Processing

Short Answer: 101
Answer & Explanation: 198

Q-102:   Why is a calibration order type a required entry in planning a calibration inspection? Select all that apply.

A. Determines inspection type

B. Record of inspection results

C. Determines order category

D. Determines the quality costs settlement rule

Short Answer: 102

Answer & Explanation: 199

Q-103:   The maintenance tasks to be performed on a due date are determined by what?

A. Maintenance task list

B. Maintenance plan

C. Maintenance strategy

Short Answer: 102
Answer & Explanation: 200

Q-104:   Which of the following is an element of the structure of a maintenance task list? Select all that apply.

A. Operation

B. Sub-operation

C. Work Center

D. Characteristic

E. Materials for maintenance work

Short Answer: 102
Answer & Explanation: 201

Q-105:   The system does not trigger the execution of an activity by a third party in relation to a calibration inspection as expected. What should be evaluated to correct this error? Select all that apply.

A. Maintenance order

B. Due date defined in maintenance task list assigned to maintenance item in maintenance plan

C. Due date defined in master inspection characteristic assigned to maintenance item in maintenance plan

D. Material master inspection settings

Short Answer: 102
Answer & Explanation: 202

Q-106:   What must occur to schedule a test equipment maintenance plan for the first time?

A. Equipment master record created

B. Measuring point assigned to equipment

C. Task list assigned to maintenance strategy

Short Answer: 102
Answer & Explanation: 203

Q-107:   Process notification, inspect equipment and process maintenance order are activities of what phase of a calibration inspection?

A. Planning

B. Inspection Lot Creation

C. Processing

Short Answer: 102
Answer & Explanation: 204

Q-108: Which of the following is a prerequisite that's performed at the application level to plan a calibration inspection? Select all that apply.

A. Create inspection type

B. Create master inspection characteristic

C. Create equipment master record

Short Answer: 102
Answer & Explanation: 204

Q-109: How are maintenance objects defined for a calibration inspection?

A. Maintenance plan item

B. Maintenance task list operation

C. Maintenance strategy

Short Answer: 102
Answer & Explanation: 205

Q-110: Test equipment is categorized by the classification system on what basis?

A. Technical specifications

B. Technical objects

C. Inspection specifications

Short Answer: 102
Answer & Explanation: 206

Q-111:   Which of the following can be used to minimize the effort required to create a maintenance task list?

A. General maintenance task list

B. General maintenance order

C. General maintenance master characteristic

D. General maintenance inspection characteristic

Short Answer: 102
Answer & Explanation: 207

Q-112:   When you create measuring points for test equipment, what's required to record quantitative measurement results?

A. Assignment of a class characteristic with the required unit of measure to the measuring point

B. Assignment of qualitative characteristic with selected set to measuring point

C.   Class characteristic assigned to measuring point and quantitative characteristic

Short Answer: 102
Answer & Explanation: 208

Q-113:   How is a calibration inspection planned and performed without a maintenance plan?

A. Maintenance order

B. Maintenance strategy

C. Maintenance task list

Short Answer: 102
Answer & Explanation: 208

Q-114: What is the result of scheduling a test equipment maintenance plan?

A. Maintenance task list includes maintenance calls that are released on due date

B. Maintenance plan includes maintenance calls that are released on due date

C. Maintenance strategy includes maintenance calls that are released on due date

Short Answer: 102
Answer & Explanation: 209

Q-115: Which of the following is a valid means to plan a sequence of calibration inspections on a performance-basis? Select all that apply.

A. Multiple-counter plan

B. Time-based maintenance plan with maintenance strategy

C. Single-cycle time-based maintenance plan

D. Performance-based maintenance plan with maintenance strategy

E. Single-cycle performance-based maintenance plan

Short Answer: 102
Answer & Explanation: 210

Q-116:   How do you ensure the appropriate materials and resources that are required to perform maintenance work are available?

A. Maintenance task list

B. Maintenance order

C. Maintenance strategy

D. Inspection characteristic

Short Answer: 103
Answer & Explanation: 212

Q-117:   A series of inspection lots have been created. However, they do not appear to have been created at the correct points in time. What might be the source of this error?

A. Definition of maintenance dates in the maintenance plan

B. Definition of maintenance dates in the maintenance strategy

C. Definition of maintenance dates in the maintenance task list

Short Answer: 103
Answer & Explanation: 213

Q-118:   Which of the following is a Customizing requirement that enables an inspection lot to be automatically generated when a maintenance order is released? Select all that apply.

A. Inspection type

B. Equipment master record

C. Order type

D. Assign inspection type to inspection point

Short Answer: 103
Answer & Explanation: 214

Q-119:   What is the purpose of a maintenance item in a maintenance plan? Select all that apply.

A. Defines maintenance object

B. Defines maintenance task list

C. Defines maintenance strategy

Short Answer: 103
Answer & Explanation: 215

Q-120:   A multiple-counter plan refers to what?

A. The use of both time- and performance-based maintenance cycles to determine maintenance dates for maintenance plan items

B. The use of both time- and performance-based maintenance cycles to determine maintenance dates for maintenance task list operations

C. The use of both time- and performance-based maintenance cycles to determine maintenance dates for maintenance order items

Short Answer: 103
Answer & Explanation: 216

Q-121:   What is the significance of the assignment of an order type to a QM inspection type?

A. Enables the creation of inspection lot when maintenance order is generated

B. Enables the creation of maintenance order when inspection lot is generated

C. Enables the creation of maintenance order when task list is created

Short Answer: 103
Answer & Explanation: 217

Q-122:   What would you use to monitor the execution of the tasks of a calibration inspection?

A. Equipment master record

B. Maintenance strategy

C. Maintenance task list

Short Answer: 103
Answer & Explanation: 218

Q-123:   Equipment maintenance cycles are defined where?

A. Maintenance plan

B. Maintenance strategy

C. Maintenance order

Short Answer: 103
Answer & Explanation: 218

Q-124: What is used to implement a time-based maintenance cycle?

A. Time-based maintenance plan with maintenance strategy

B. Performance-based maintenance plan with maintenance strategy

C. Multiple-counter plan

D. Single-cycle time-based maintenance plan

E. Single-cycle performance-based maintenance plan

Short Answer: 103
Answer & Explanation: 219

Q-125: Which of the following can be specified for a maintenance plan for calibration inspections? Select all that apply.

A. Scheduling parameter

B. Task list

C. Maintenance order

D. Master inspection characteristics

E. Maintenance plan category

Short Answer: 103
Answer & Explanation: 220

Q-126: The customer wants to enter quantitative measurement results for a measurement point for test equipment. What assignment is required to do so?

A. Assign qualitative characteristic to measuring point

B. Assign class characteristic to measuring point

C. Assign quantitative characteristic to measuring point

Short Answer: 103
Answer & Explanation: 221

Q-127: How do you ensure that test equipment is inspected and calibrated on the basis of use?

A. Time-based maintenance plan with maintenance strategy

B. Performance-based maintenance plan with maintenance strategy

C. Multiple-counter plan

D. Single-cycle time-based maintenance plan

E. Single-cycle performance-based maintenance plan

Short Answer: 103
Answer & Explanation: 222

Q-128: What entry is required to create a single cycle plan for a calibration inspection?

A. Unit of measure for the maintenance cycle

B. Equipment master record

C. Maintenance plan category

Short Answer: 104
Answer & Explanation: 223

Q-129: Which of the following is a prerequisite to a calibration inspection at the application level if measurement documents will be updated with inspection results in Plant Maintenance?

A. Creation of master inspection characteristic

B. Creation of function location

C. Creation of task list

D. Assignment of master inspection characteristics to operations

E. Creation of maintenance plan

Short Answer: 104
Answer & Explanation: 224

Q-130: What is used to define the maintenance object to be maintained using a calibration inspection?

A. Maintenance plan

B. Maintenance strategy

C. Maintenance task list

Short Answer: 104
Answer & Explanation: 225

Q-131: The point at which maintenance tasks related to calibration equipment are performed is incorrect. How can this issue be corrected? Select all that apply.

A. Review measurement point defined in the IMG for the calibration inspection

B. Review the scheduling parameters defined for the maintenance plan

C. Review the maintenance strategy defined for the maintenance plan

C. All of the above

D. None of the above

Short Answer: 104
Answer & Explanation: 226

Q-132:   Where are the settings made that define the maintenance tasks to be performed on a due date ?

A. Maintenance plan

B. Maintenance task list

C. Maintenance strategy

D. Inspection lot

Short Answer: 104
Answer & Explanation: 226

Q-133:   Which of the following is an application requirement that enables an inspection lot to be automatically generated when a maintenance order is released?

A. Create maintenance plan

B. Create inspection characteristic

C. Assign task list to maintenance plan

Short Answer: 104
Answer & Explanation: 227

Q-134: The user wants to ensure calibration inspections occur on time, rather than performance-based intervals. How is this objective met?

A. Maintenance cycles in maintenance plan

B. Maintenance cycles in maintenance strategy

C. Maintenance cycles in maintenance task list

Short Answer: 104
Answer & Explanation: 228

Q-135: What step is required to create a calibration inspection time-based strategy plan?

A. Assign task list to maintenance order

B. Enter maintenance plan category

C. Enter performance-based maintenance strategy

Short Answer: 104
Answer & Explanation: 229

Q-136: How do you ensure that a calibration inspection is triggered by a series of measuring points?

A. Performance-based maintenance plan

B. Time-based maintenance plan

C. Multiple-counter plan

D. Single-cycle time-based maintenance plan

Short Answer: 104
Answer & Explanation: 230

Q-137:   The customer wants to change the point at which a maintenance task is performed during the calibration inspection. Where is this change made? Select all that apply.

A. Maintenance task list

B. Maintenance plan

C. Maintenance order

Short Answer: 104
Answer & Explanation: 231

Q-138:   What statement is applicable to the definition of a maintenance plan? Select all that apply.

A. Identifies maintenance object that's the subject of the maintenance tasks

B. Maintenance strategy must be used

C. Consists of maintenance items for which the maintenance objects and maintenance task list are defined

D. Contains due date of the maintenance item as determined by the maintenance task list assigned to the maintenance item

E. Due date of maintenance item leads to the generation of a maintenance or service order

Short Answer: 104
Answer & Explanation: 232

Q-139:   The customer requires the ability to plan maintenance tasks, monitor the completion of the tasks and account for the costs incurred to perform the tasks. What will enable them to do so?

A. Maintenance task list

B. Maintenance strategy

C. Maintenance order

Short Answer: 104
Answer & Explanation: 233

Q-140:   What option is available to plan the inspection and maintenance tasks for a maintenance object? Select all that apply.

A. Time-based maintenance plan with maintenance strategy

B. Time and performance-based maintenance plan with maintenance strategy

C. Performance-based single-cycle plan with maintenance strategy

Short Answer: 105
Answer & Explanation: 234

Q-141:   Equipment status update and change cycle modification factor are examples of what?

A. Calibration inspection planning function

B. Calibration inspection follow-up function

C. Calibration inspection lot creation function

Short Answer: 105
Answer & Explanation: 235

Q-142: A maintenance object is assigned to which of the following?

A. Maintenance item in maintenance plan

B. Operation in task list

C. Maintenance item in maintenance strategy

Short Answer: 105
Answer & Explanation: 236

Q-143: Why are measuring points important in test equipment management?

A. Parameter used to define maintenance plan

B. Parameter used to define maintenance strategy

C. Parameter used to define maintenance task list

Short Answer: 105
Answer & Explanation: 237

Q-144: The customer wants to structure maintenance cycles on both a time and performance basis. What is required to do so?

A. Maintenance strategy

B. Maintenance plan

C. Maintenance task list

Short Answer: 105

Answer & Explanation: 238

Q-145:   Why is a task list assigned to a maintenance item in a maintenance plan?

A. Record results of inspection

B. Describe maintenance strategy to be performed on individual due dates

C. Define the maintenance tasks to be performed on individual due dates

D. Define PRT used to maintain equipment

Short Answer: 105
Answer & Explanation: 239

Q-146:   What types of maintenance plans without a maintenance strategy are available? Select all that apply.

A. Time-based single cycle plan

B. Performance-based single cycle plan

C. Multiple-counter plan

D. All of the above

E. None of the above

Short Answer: 105
Answer & Explanation: 240

Q-147:   The customer requires the ability to immediately determine if a piece of test equipment is released for use in an inspection. What should be referenced to do so?

A. Maintenance plan

B. Maintenance order

C. Equipment master record

Short Answer: 105
Answer & Explanation: 241

Q-148: What would you use to define the maintenance object to be maintained and the task list to be used for a calibration inspection?

A. Maintenance plan

B. Maintenance strategy

C. Maintenance cycle

D. Maintenance schedule

Short Answer: 105
Answer & Explanation: 241

Q-149: What would you use to define maintenance dates for test equipment on either a time and performance basis?

A. Maintenance strategy

B. Maintenance plan

C. Maintenance schedule

Short Answer: 105
Answer & Explanation: 242

Q-150: What types of maintenance plans with maintenance strategy are available? Select all that apply.

A. Time-based maintenance plan with maintenance strategy

B. Performance-based maintenance plan with maintenance strategy

D. Multiple-counter maintenance plan

E. Time-based single cycle maintenance plan

E. Performance-based single cycle maintenance plan

Short Answer: 105
Answer & Explanation: 244

Q-151: The creation of an inspection lot for a calibration inspection does not occur as expected on each of a sequence of dates. What may be the origin of this error? Select all that apply.

A. Maintenance plan not defined

B. Definition of maintenance task list assigned to maintenance item in maintenance plan

C. Issue with the maintenance plan schedule

Short Answer: 105
Answer & Explanation: 245

Q-152: The customer wants to structure a maintenance plan with reference to time. What can be used to do so? Select all that apply.

A. Maintenance plan with maintenance strategy

B. Single cycle plan

C. Maintenance plan without maintenance strategy

Short Answer: 105
Answer & Explanation: 246

Q-153: What is the purpose of the creation of measuring points for test equipment? Select all that apply.

A. Measure the wear rate to a piece of test equipment

B. Input to performance-based maintenance plan

C. Input to time-based maintenance plan

Short Answer: 106
Answer & Explanation: 247

Q-154: Which of the following is a standard inspection type that's defined for a calibration inspection?

A. PM05

B. PD30

C. PL04

Short Answer: 106
Answer & Explanation: 247

Q-155: What is the purpose of the assignment of a maintenance task list to a maintenance plan?

A. Determines the tasks to be performed on a due date

B. Determines the maintenance objects to be maintained

C. Determines the maintenance schedule

Short Answer: 106
Answer & Explanation: 248

Q-156: The customer wants to plan a calibration inspection. What is required at the application level to do so? Select all that apply.

A. Creation of inspection characteristics

B. Creation of maintenance plan

C. Creation of material master record

D. Creation of task list

E. Creation of measurement documents

Short Answer: 106
Answer & Explanation: 249

Q-157: The customer wants to perform maintenance and inspection tasks for test equipment on a calendar or performance basis. What enables him to do so?

A. Maintenance plan with maintenance strategy

B. Maintenance plan without maintenance strategy

C. Single-cycle plan

D. All of the above

E. None of the above

Q-158:   The customer wants to perform maintenance and inspection tasks for test equipment on a performance basis. What enables him to do so? Select all that apply.

A. Performance-based maintenance plan with maintenance strategy

B. Performance-based maintenance plan without maintenance strategy

C. Performance-based single cycle plan

Q-159:   The object used to define the maintenance and inspection tasks to be performed on test equipment as well the dates the tasks are to be performed is referred to as what?

A. Maintenance strategy

B. Maintenance plan

C. Maintenance task list

Q-160:   What is used to define the scope of the maintenance tasks to be performed on test equipment?

A. Maintenance strategy

B. Maintenance plan

C. Maintenance task list

Short Answer: 106
Answer & Explanation: 253

Q-161: What is a requirement for the creation of measuring points for test equipment? Select all that apply.

A. Measuring point categories

B. Assignment of class characteristics to measuring points

C. Single cycle performance-based plan

D. All of the above

E. None of the above

Short Answer: 106
Answer & Explanation: 254

Q-162: A maintenance plan structure consists of what elements? Select all that apply.

A. Maintenance orders

B. Maintenance items

C. Maintenance operations

Short Answer: 106
Answer & Explanation: 255

Q-163: The maintenance intervals defined in the equipment master record for test equipment are defined on what basis? Select all that apply.

A. Equipment usage

B. Inspection points

C. Time schedule

Short Answer: 106
Answer & Explanation: 256

Q-164: What is required to update measurement documents on the basis of calibration inspection results?

A. Create inspection characteristic

B. Crease measuring point characteristic/counter with reference to class characteristic

C. Assign measuring point or counter to test equipment

Short Answer: 106
Answer & Explanation: 257

Q-165: What is a maintenance plan maintenance item?

A. Defines maintenance strategy

B. Defines maintenance object

C. Defines maintenance task list

Short Answer: 107

Answer & Explanation: 258

Q-166:   Identify an effect of the occurrence of a due date defined in a time-based maintenance plan.

A. Creation of maintenance or service order

B. Creation of maintenance cycle

C. Creation of calibration inspection intervals

Short Answer: 107
Answer & Explanation: 259

Q-167:   What must be created in order for inspection operations defined in a maintenance task list to be performed by a third party?

A. Order

B. Operation

C. Maintenance plan

D. Maintenance strategy

Short Answer: 107
Answer & Explanation: 260

Q-168:   In relation to a calibration inspection, why is a maintenance or service order generated for a maintenance due date? Select all that apply.

A. Monitor execution of maintenance tasks

B. Plan maintenance tasks

C. Settlement of costs incurred by performance of maintenance tasks

D. All of the above

E. None of the above

Short Answer: 107
Answer & Explanation: 261

Q-169:   Which of the following can be included in the structure of an inspection lot created for a calibration inspection? Select all that apply.

A. Operation to define the activity to be performed at a work center

B. Inspection characteristic to define the focus of the inspection

C. Sample size defined for characteristic

D. Conditions for acceptance or rejection of inspection lot

E. Inspection points

F. PRT required for operation

Short Answer: 107
Answer & Explanation: 262

Q-170:   The system does not allow the automatic update of measurement documents as a follow-up action for the inspection lot. What is a solution?

A. Define measuring points to record results for piece of test equipment

B. Define inspection intervals for maintenance plans

C. Link master inspection characteristic to measuring points

Short Answer: 107
Answer & Explanation: 263

Q-171:   You want to update the measurement documents automatically after a calibration inspection. What is required to do so? Select all that apply.

A. Assignment of measuring point to equipment master record

B. Creation of measuring point characteristic with reference to class characteristic

C. Creation of maintenance task list

Short Answer: 107
Answer & Explanation: 264

Q-172:   What function must be completed for a measurement document to be automatically updated as a follow-up action for a calibration inspection?

A. Defects Recording

B. Results Recording

C. Usage Decision

Short Answer: 107
Answer & Explanation: 264

Q-173:   What is used to monitor equipment calibration dates?

A. Maintenance schedule

B. Maintenance order

C. Maintenance task list

Short Answer: 107
Answer & Explanation: 265

Q-174: The maintenance schedule used to monitor calibration dates is created on what basis? Select all that apply.

A. Time-based maintenance schedule

B. Performance-based maintenance schedule

C. Time and performance-based maintenance schedule

D. All of the above

E. None of the above

Short Answer: 107
Answer & Explanation: 266

Q-175: Which of the following is the standard inspection type that's defined for a calibration inspection?

A. I4

B. PM05

C. QL05F

Short Answer: 107
Answer & Explanation: 267

Q-176: When you create measuring points for test equipment, what is required to record qualitative measurement results?

A. Assignment of qualitative characteristic with selected set to measuring point

B. Creation of master inspection characteristics

C. Assignment of class characteristic and master inspection characteristic to measuring point/counter

Short Answer: 107
Answer & Explanation: 268

Q-177: You create a maintenance task list. What is required to update measurement documents on the basis of calibration inspection results?

A. Creation of equipment master record

B. Creation of inspection characteristic

C. Assignment of measuring point or counter to equipment master record

Short Answer: 108
Answer & Explanation: 269

Q-178: Which of the following entries are required to create a single cycle maintenance plan? Select all that apply.

A. Maintenance plan category

B. Scheduling parameters for the maintenance plan

C. Time-based maintenance strategy

D. Task list

E. Maintenance packages

Short Answer: 108
Answer & Explanation: 269

Q-179:   What must occur to schedule a test equipment maintenance plan for the first time?

A. Assign task list to maintenance plan

B. Create inspection characteristic

C. Create equipment master record

Short Answer: 108
Answer & Explanation: 270

Q-180:   Scheduling a maintenance plan is a function of what application?

A. Plant Maintenance

B. Quality Management

C. Production Planning

Short Answer: 108
Answer & Explanation: 271

Q-181:   A release of a test equipment maintenance call in a maintenance plan leads to what?

A. Creation of maintenance order

B. Creation of inspection lot

C. Creation of start of cycle for maintenance plan

Short Answer: 108
Answer & Explanation: 272

Q-182:   What must occur to automatically reschedule a test equipment performance-based maintenance plan?

A. Creation of order for maintenance plan

B. Confirmation of last due date

C. Confirmation of maintenance plan counter

Short Answer: 108
Answer & Explanation: 273

Q-183:   What is the purpose of measurement points/counters that are defined for test equipment?

A. Measure depreciation of test equipment

B. Confirm last maintenance due date

C. Trigger recalculation of maintenance calls

Short Answer: 108
Answer & Explanation: 274

Q-184:   What is defined in a test equipment maintenance plan item?

A. Maintenance object

B. Maintenance order

C. Maintenance task list

Short Answer: 108
Answer & Explanation: 274

Q-185: What is a requirement to plan and perform a calibration inspection without a maintenance plan?

A. Assign inspection type to maintenance order type

B. Assign measuring point to equipment master record

C. Assign class characteristic to measuring point

Short Answer: 108
Answer & Explanation: 276

Q-186: The customer requires the ability to describe the work steps of a calibration inspection. Which of the following enables him to do so?

A. Maintenance order

B. Maintenance task list

C. Maintenance strategy

Short Answer: 108
Answer & Explanation: 276

Q-187: What is used to document maintenance tasks and define the work center at which the tasks will be performed?

A. Maintenance strategy

B. Maintenance task list

C. Maintenance order

Short Answer: 108
Answer & Explanation: 277

Q-188: A maintenance strategy or maintenance cycle is used for what purpose in relation to a calibration inspection?

A. Define inspection interval

B. Define inspection point

C. Define inspection type

Short Answer: 108
Answer & Explanation: 278

Q-189: A maintenance cycle can be_____? Select all that apply.

A. Created at the maintenance plan level

B. Valid for all operations in a task list

C. Time or performance based

Short Answer: 108
Answer & Explanation: 279

Q-190: A maintenance object and maintenance task list are defined in which of the following?

A. Master strategy

B. Maintenance plan

C. Maintenance order

Short Answer: 108

Answer & Explanation: 280

Q-191:   Which of the following is a true statement regarding a maintenance order? Select all that apply.

A. Triggered by the maintenance plan

B. Determines maintenance tasks to be performed on due date

C. Structured with regard to time or performance

Short Answer: 109
Answer & Explanation: 281

Q-192:   Which of the following describes a maintenance task list? Select all that apply.

A. Created in Quality Management

B. Activities performed to maintain maintenance objects

C.   Master inspection characteristics can be assigned to task list sub-operations

Short Answer: 109
Answer & Explanation: 282

Q-193:   Which of the following statements pertain to a maintenance plan? Select all that apply.

A. Central planning object

B. Assigned to maintenance task list

C. Requires inspection type which allows the automatic creation of maintenance order and inspection lot

Short Answer: 109
Answer & Explanation: 283

Q-194: What is the purpose of test equipment tracking? Select all that apply.

A. Determine the inspection lots that were inspected using a particular piece of test equipment

B. Determine the inspection characteristics that were inspected using a particular piece of test equipment

C. Determine the inspection operations that were performed with a particular piece of test equipment

Short Answer: 109
Answer & Explanation: 284

Q-195: What is a requirement to plan a calibration inspection at the Customizing level?

A. Assignment of inspection type to maintenance order type

B. Creation of maintenance plan

C. Definition of default values for inspection type

Short Answer: 109
Answer & Explanation: 285

Q-196: Master inspection characteristics are linked to classification characteristics for what purpose in relation to a calibration inspection?

A. Record inspection results for measurement points of test equipment using measurement documents

B. Schedule calibration inspection for maintenance order

C. Record inspection results for measurement points in equipment master record results history

Short Answer: 109
Answer & Explanation: 286

Q-197:   A maintenance cycle can be defined on what basis for a calibration inspection? Select all that apply.

A. Time

B. Performance

C. Combination time and performance

D. All of the above

E. None of the above

Short Answer: 109
Answer & Explanation: 286

Q-198:   Which of the following is a true statement regarding the Test Equipment Management component?

A. Test equipment maintenance history is maintained in the equipment master record

B. QM maintenance processing is an application that is integrated with the test equipment management component

C. Test equipment cannot be grouped for inspection processing

Short Answer: 109
Answer & Explanation: 287

Q-199:   Identify a follow-up action that is executed following the entry of a usage decision for a calibration inspection lot.

A. Change cycle modification factor

B. Create measuring points with reference to class characteristics

C. Release maintenance order

Short Answer: 109
Answer & Explanation: 288

Q-200:   Which of the following is required to enter qualitative measurement results for a measuring point for test equipment?

A. Assign class characteristic with selected set to measuring point

B. Assign qualitative characteristic with a selected set to measuring point

C. Assign class characteristic with unit of measure to measuring point

D. Assign quality characteristic with unit of measure to measuring point

Short Answer: 109
Answer & Explanation: 289

Q-201: Which of the following is a valid calibration inspection follow-up function? Select all that apply.

A. Schedule maintenance plan

B. Change cycle modification factor

C. Create maintenance strategy

D. Update equipment status

E. Create measuring points

Short Answer: 109
Answer & Explanation: 289

CHAPTER II

SHORT ANSWERS

SHORT ANSWERS

Q-1:   A. Inspect and calibrate test equipment used to perform quality inspections, B. Manage the inspection and maintenance of test equipment using equipment master records and D. Schedule calibration inspections per maintenance orders and maintenance strategies

Q-2:   A. Update status in equipment master record and C. Update cycle modification factor

Q-3:   B. Create inspection lot

Q-4:   B. Maintenance plan

Q-5:   A. Equipment task list, C. General maintenance task list and D. Functional location task list

Q-6:   A. Equipment master record

Q-7:   C. Quality characteristic with selected set was not assigned to the measuring point

Q-8:   C. Class characteristic is assigned to measuring point and master inspection characteristic

Q-9:   A. Define maintenance object and C. Define maintenance task list

Q-10: A. Provides the means to manage test equipment at the client level and C. Provides the means to document the maintenance history of test equipment

Q-11: A. Single-cycle plan and C. Multiple-counter plan

Q-12: A. Creation of inspection lot

Q-13: A. Single-cycle plan

Q-14: A. The general maintenance task list is not linked to a maintenance object and B. The general maintenance task list serves as a proposal during the creation of maintenance order or maintenance task list

Q-15: C. Maintenance order

Q-16: A. Point at which inspection tasks are performed is determined by counter readings

Q-17: C. Schedule maintenance plan

Q-18: A. Plant Maintenance - Maintenance Processing, B. Plant Maintenance - Preventive Maintenance and E. Quality Management - Inspections

Q-19: B. Classification System

Q-20: A. Plant Maintenance

Q-21:   A. Change valuation mode

Q-22:   A. Time-based maintenance plan with maintenance strategy, B. Performance-based maintenance plan with maintenance strategy, D. Time-based single cycle maintenance plan and E. Performance-based single cycle maintenance plan

Q-23:   A. Operation and B. Sub-operation

Q-24:   A. Maintenance order

Q-25:   C. Characteristic with selected set not assigned to measuring point

Q-26:   B. Equipment master record and C. Task list

Q-27:   A. Equipment usage and B. Time schedule

Q-28:   A. Measuring point categories and C. Assignment of class characteristics with unit of measure to measuring points

Q-29:   A. Equipment task list and B. General task list

Q-30:   A. Plant Maintenance

Q-31:   A. Maintenance plan

Q-32:   B. Maintenance task list

Q-33:   A. QM Test Equipment Management

Q-34:   C. Equipment master record

Q-35:   B. Linkage of the master inspection characteristic to class characteristic in the classification system

Q-36:   A. Activities of the planning phase of a calibration inspection

Q-37:   C. Maintenance plan

Q-38:   A. May consist of operations and sub-operations, B. May be an equipment, functional location or general maintenance task list and D. The operation can be performed by internal or external partner

Q-39:   B. Plan maintenance work to be performed at a particular work center and C. Settle costs of test equipment maintenance

Q-40:   A. Creation and release of maintenance order

Q-41:   A. Inspection type and C. Order type

Q-42:   A. Record inspection results for measuring points using measurement documents

Q-43:   C. Define inspection points

Q-44:   A. Test Equipment Management: Create Measuring Point for Equipment and B. Test

Equipment Management: Edit Equipment
Master Record

Q-45:   C. Link master inspection characteristics to
         class characteristics using the classification
         system and D. Define inspection
         specifications for both quantitative and
         qualitative characteristics

Q-46:   A. Create Maintenance Task List and B.
         Create Test Equipment Master Record

Q-47:   A. Usage Decision

Q-48:   A. Create measuring point for equipment and
         B. Edit equipment master record

Q-49:   B. Equipment task list and C. Functional
         location task list

Q-50:   A. Maintenance order

Q-51:   A. Resource

Q-52:   B. Maintenance task list

Q-53:   B. Enter equipment key and C. Enter test
         equipment category

Q-54:   A. Class characteristic is assigned to the
         master inspection characteristic and measuring
         point/counter and B. Master inspection
         characteristics

Q-55:   B. Inspection can be conducted

Q-56:   C. Define task list, D. Link master inspection
        characteristics to inspection characteristics in
        the classification system and E. Define
        maintenance strategy

Q-57:   B. Define inspection type and C. Define order
        type

Q-58:   B. Assign class characteristic to measuring
        point

Q-59:   A. Plant Maintenance

Q-60:   A. Plant Maintenance Information System and
        B. Quality Management Information System

Q-61:   B. Maintenance task list

Q-62:   A. Tasks of maintenance task list are
        scheduled on a calendar basis

Q-63:   A. Inspection type and B. Inspection points

Q-64:   C. Maintenance order

Q-65:   A. Assignment of task list to maintenance plan
        and B. Assignment of inspection
        characteristics to operations

Q-66: A. Incorrect class characteristic unit of measure and B. Incorrect class characteristic assigned to measuring point

Q-67: B. Measuring point assigned to equipment

Q-68: A. Plant Maintenance - Preventive Maintenance, B. Plant Maintenance – Maintenance Processing and D. Quality Management - Quality Inspections

Q-69: B. Schedule maintenance plan and D. Create maintenance plan for maintenance strategy

Q-70: A. Maintenance plan may be defined with or without a maintenance strategy and B. Maintenance plan may be time- and/or performance-based

Q-71: B. Maintenance plan

Q-72: B. Equipment master record, C. Task list and D. Maintenance plan

Q-73: A. The maintenance strategy enables a time-based or performance-based maintenance plan to be executed on a recurring basis

Q-74: A. Maintenance cycle defined for a maintenance plan

Q-75: C. Schedule maintenance plan

Q-76: A. Create task list and C. Create measuring points, counters and measurement documents

Q-77: A. Record Results

Q-78: C. Sampling procedure

Q-79: A. Valuation mode

Q-80: A. Performance

Q-81: B. Maintenance plan

Q-82: B. Define the individual steps of a calibration inspection in greater detail than would be possible if an operation were used

Q–83: C. Maintenance order

Q-84: B. Inspection lot is to be created automatically as a maintenance order is released

Q-85: B. Class characteristic is not assigned to measuring point/counter and master inspection characteristic

Q-86: B. Maintenance task list

Q-87: B. Maintenance task list

Q-88: A. Plant Maintenance

Q-89:   A. Update equipment status and E. Update measurement documents

Q-90:   B. Time-based maintenance plan with maintenance strategy and C. Single-cycle time-based maintenance plan

Q-91:   A. Materials assigned to maintenance task list operation and C. Master inspection characteristic assigned to operation

Q-92:   C. Inspection characteristic

Q-93:   B. Assign qualitative characteristic with a selected set to the measuring point

Q-94:   A. Equipment master record

Q-95:   A. Test equipment

Q-96:   B. Time-based maintenance plan with maintenance strategy

Q-97:   C. Maintenance order

Q-98:   E. Any of the above

Q-99:   A. Operations are performed in chronological order

Q-100: A. Operation in maintenance task list

Q-101: A. Planning

Q-102: D. Determines the quality costs settlement
rule

Q-103: B. Maintenance plan

Q-104: A. Operation and B. Sub-operation

Q-105: A. Maintenance order

Q-106: A. Equipment master record created

Q-107: C. Processing

Q-108: B. Create master inspection characteristic and
C. Create equipment master record

Q-109: A. Maintenance plan item

Q-110: A. Technical specifications

Q-111: A. General maintenance task list

Q-112: A. Assignment of a class characteristic with
the required unit of measure to the measuring
point

Q-113: A. Maintenance order

Q-114: B. Maintenance plan includes maintenance
calls that are released on due date

Q-115: D. Performance-based maintenance plan with
maintenance strategy

Q-116: A. Maintenance task list

Q-117: A. Definition of maintenance dates in the maintenance plan

Q-118: A. Inspection type and C. Order type

Q-119: A. Defines maintenance object and B. Defines maintenance task list

Q-120: A. The use of both time- and performance-based maintenance cycles to determine maintenance dates for maintenance plan items

Q-121: A. Enables the creation of inspection lot when maintenance order is generated

Q-122: A. Equipment master record

Q-123: A. Maintenance plan

Q-124: A. Time-based maintenance plan with maintenance strategy

Q-125: A. Scheduling parameter, B. Task list and E. Maintenance plan category

Q-126: B. Assign class characteristic to measuring point

Q-127: B. Performance-based maintenance plan with maintenance strategy and E. Single-cycle performance-based maintenance plan

Q-128: A. Unit of measure for the maintenance cycle and C. Maintenance plan category

Q-129: A. Creation of master inspection characteristic, C. Creation of task list and E. Creation of maintenance plan

Q-130: A. Maintenance plan

Q-131: D. All of the above

Q-132: A. Maintenance plan

Q-133: A. Create maintenance plan and C. Assign task list to maintenance plan

Q-134: A. Maintenance cycles in maintenance plan

Q-135: B. Enter maintenance plan category

Q-136: A. Performance-based maintenance plan

Q-137: B. Maintenance plan

Q-138: A. Identifies maintenance object that's the subject of the maintenance tasks and C. Consists of maintenance items for which the maintenance objects and maintenance task list are defined

Q-139: C. Maintenance order

Q-140:   A. Time-based maintenance plan with maintenance strategy

Q-141:   B. Calibration inspection follow-up function

Q-142:   A. Maintenance item in maintenance plan

Q-143:   A. Parameter used to define maintenance plan

Q-144:   B. Maintenance plan

Q-145:   C. Define the maintenance tasks to be performed on individual due dates

Q-146:   D. All of the above

Q-147:   C. Equipment master record

Q-148:   A. Maintenance plan

Q-149:   B. Maintenance plan

Q-150:   A. Time-based maintenance plan with maintenance strategy, B. Performance-based maintenance plan with maintenance strategy and D. Time-based single-cycle maintenance plan

Q-151:   A. Maintenance plan not defined

Q-152:   A. Maintenance plan with maintenance strategy and B. Single cycle plan

Q-153: A. Measure the wear rate to a piece of test equipment and B. Input to performance-based maintenance plan

Q-154: A. PM05

Q-155: A. Determines the specific tasks to be performed on a due date

Q-156: B. Creation of maintenance plan and D. Creation of task list

Q-157: A. Maintenance plan with maintenance strategy

Q-158: A. Performance-based maintenance plan with maintenance strategy

Q-159: B. Maintenance plan

Q-160: B. Maintenance plan

Q-161: A. Measuring point categories and B. Assignment of class characteristics to measuring points

Q-162: B. Maintenance items

Q-163: A. Equipment usage and C. Time schedule

Q-164: B. Create measuring point characteristic/counter with reference to class characteristic and C. Assign measuring point or counter to test equipment

Q-165: B. Defines maintenance object and C. Defines maintenance task list

Q-166: A. Creation of maintenance or service order

Q-167: A. Order

Q-168: D. All of the above

Q-169: A. Operation to define the activity to be performed at a work center

Q-170: A. Define measuring points to record results for piece of test equipment and C. Link master inspection characteristic to measuring points

Q-171: A. Assignment of measuring point to equipment master record and B. Creation of measuring point characteristic with reference to class characteristic

Q-172: C. Usage Decision

Q-173: A. Maintenance schedule

Q-174: A. Time-based maintenance schedule and B. Performance-based maintenance schedule

Q-175: B. PM05

Q-176: A. Assignment of qualitative characteristic with selected set to measuring point

Q-177: C. Assignment of measuring point or counter to equipment master record

Q-178: A. Maintenance plan category and B. Scheduling parameters for the maintenance plan

Q-179: A. Assign task list to maintenance plan and C. Create equipment master record

Q-180: B. Quality Management

Q-181: B. Creation of inspection lot

Q-182: C. Confirmation of maintenance plan counter

Q-183: A. Measure depreciation of test equipment

Q-184: A. Maintenance object and C. Maintenance task list

Q-185: A. Assign inspection type to maintenance order type

Q-186: B. Maintenance task list

Q-187: B. Maintenance task list

Q-188: A. Define inspection interval

Q-189: A. Created at the maintenance plan level and C. Time or performance based

Q-190: B. Maintenance plan

Q-191: A. Triggered by the maintenance plan

Q-192: B. Activities performed to maintain maintenance objects

Q-193: A. Central planning object

Q-194: A. Determine the inspection lots that were inspected using a particular piece of test equipment and B. Determine the inspection characteristics that were inspected using a particular piece of test equipment

Q-195: A. Assignment of inspection type to maintenance order type

Q-196: A. Record inspection results for measurement points of test equipment using measurement documents

Q-197: D. All of the above

Q-198: A. Test equipment maintenance history is maintained in the equipment master record

Q-199: A. Change cycle modification factor

Q-200: B. Assign qualitative characteristic with a selected set to measuring point

Q-201: B. Change cycle modification factor

CHAPTER III

ANSWERS & EXPLANATIONS

ANSWERS & EXPLANATIONS

Q-1:   A. Inspect and calibrate test equipment used to perform quality inspections, B. Manage the inspection and maintenance of test equipment using equipment master records and D. Schedule calibration inspections per maintenance orders and maintenance strategies

Test equipment is regularly inspected and calibrated to ensure it adheres to predefined performance criteria and is suitable for quality inspections. The results of the calibration inspection govern the release of the test equipment for subsequent use. The planning, scheduling and performance of calibration inspections require the master data, as well as the planning and processing functions of the Quality Management and Plant Maintenance components. For example, the inspection planning functions required to process a calibration inspection include creating equipment master records and test equipment groups, linking master inspection characteristics to class characteristics using the classification system and defining inspection specifications for both quantitative and qualitative characteristics. Additional planning functions include creating inspection characteristics for the maintenance task list operations and maintenance cycles in the maintenance plan, monitoring maintenance schedules and the status of the test equipment, and creating and releasing maintenance orders. In turn, the inspection processing functions include documenting inspection results for each piece of test equipment and creating maintenance notifications. valuating test equipment in an inspection lot, entering the usage decision for the inspection lot and confirming services for maintenance orders. Additional processing functions include conducting follow-up actions for an inspection lot usage decision and updating the Plant Maintenance and Quality Management Information Systems.

Q-2:   A. Update status in equipment master record and C. Update cycle modification factor

A usage decision code for an inspection lot documents the outcome of a calibration inspection and concludes the calibration inspection. On the basis of this code and its linkage to follow-up actions, individual functions can be performed automatically. One such follow-up function is the calculation of a quality score for the inspection lot. Other follow-up actions include using the cycle modification factor to update the inspection interval in the preventive maintenance plan and creating measurement documents for each measuring point to record inspection results. Additional follow-up actions include updating the status of a piece of equipment in the equipment master record to reflect the usage decision for the inspection and the technical completion of a maintenance order.

Q-3:   B. Create inspection lot

Functions of the Plant Maintenance and Quality Management components support the inspection, calibration and maintenance of test equipment to ensure it adheres to predefined performance criteria.

The planning, scheduling and performance of calibration inspections require the master data and planning and processing functions of the Test Equipment Management component. In particular, the functions required to complete the second phase of a calibration inspection -- the Inspection Lot Creation phase -- include scheduling the maintenance plan, creating and releasing the order, and creating the inspection lot.

Q-4:   B. Maintenance plan

A maintenance plan is the central planning object for a calibration inspection. Maintenance plan items control the maintenance and inspection tasks that are performed on maintenance objects. These items use maintenance cycles for which time and performance-based inspection intervals are defined to control when maintenance or inspection tasks are performed. Depending on Customizing settings, as a maintenance plan is scheduled, maintenance calls are created and converted to orders when the calls are due. As an order is released, an inspection lot is created and the maintenance task list is selected and assigned to the maintenance plan. Each task list structure contains operations and possibly sub-operations that describe the work to be performed during a calibration inspection. Inspection characteristics that describe what will be inspected using quantitative or qualitative inspection specifications can be assigned to the task list. Following the selection and assignment of the task list, the calibration inspection operations are performed in chronological order and characteristic inspection results are recorded and valuated. Next, based on the valuation of the inspection characteristics, a usage decision for the inspection lot is documented and the inspection lot is completed. The completion of the calibration inspection triggers an update to the test equipment status in the equipment master record to reflect the test equipment valuation as indicated by the lot's usage decision. In turn, the activities of the calibration inspection are confirmed for the maintenance order using either the Results Recording or Inspection Lot Completion functions.

Q-5:   A. Equipment task list, C. General maintenance task list and D. Functional location task list

A maintenance plan is the central planning object for a calibration inspection. Maintenance plan items control the maintenance and inspection tasks that are performed on maintenance objects. These items use maintenance cycles for which time and performance-based inspection intervals are defined to control when maintenance or inspection tasks are performed. Depending on Customizing settings, as a maintenance plan is scheduled, maintenance calls are created and converted to orders when the calls are due. As an order is released, an inspection lot is created and the maintenance task list is selected and assigned to the maintenance plan. Each task list structure contains operations and possibly sub-operations that describe the work to be performed during a calibration inspection. Inspection characteristics that describe what will be inspected using quantitative or qualitative inspection specifications can be assigned to the task list. Following the selection and assignment of the task list, the calibration inspection operations are performed in chronological order and characteristic inspection results are recorded and valuated. Next, based on the valuation of the inspection characteristics, a usage decision for the inspection lot is documented and the inspection lot is completed. The completion of the calibration inspection triggers an update to the test equipment status in the equipment master record to reflect the test equipment valuation as indicated by the lot's usage decision. In turn, the activities of the calibration inspection are confirmed for the maintenance order using either the Results Recording or Inspection Lot Completion functions.

Q-6:   A. Equipment master record

A usage decision code for an inspection lot documents the outcome of a calibration inspection and concludes the calibration inspection. On the basis of this code and its linkage to follow-up actions, individual functions can be performed automatically. One such follow-up function is the calculation of a quality score for the inspection lot. Other follow-up actions include using the cycle modification factor to update the inspection interval in the preventive maintenance plan and creating measurement documents for each measuring point to record inspection results. Additional follow-up actions include updating the status of a piece of equipment in the equipment master record to reflect the usage decision for the inspection and the technical completion of a maintenance order.

Q-7:   C. Qualitative characteristic with selected set
was not assigned to the measuring point

A usage decision code for an inspection lot concludes
an inspection and documents its outcome. On the
basis of this code and its linkage to follow-up functions,
the functions can be executed automatically. One such
follow-up action is the creation of measurement
documents to record inspection results for each
inspection point that's defined for the test equipment.
The critical values obtained by measurement readings
are recorded in the documents and used to monitor a
technical installation. The measurement documents are
stored in the test equipment master record. The
requirements for this functionality include the linkage
of master inspection characteristics in the maintenance
task list to measuring point master records by means of
the class characteristics, as well as the creation of
measuring point categories. Also required is the
assignment of qualitative characteristics to measuring
points.

Q-8:   C. Class characteristic is assigned to measuring
point and master inspection characteristic

A usage decision code for an inspection lot concludes
an inspection and documents its outcome. On the
basis of this code and its linkage to follow-up functions,
the functions can be executed automatically. One such
follow-up action is the creation of measurement
documents to record inspection results for each
inspection point that's defined for the test equipment.
The critical values obtained by measurement readings
are recorded in the documents and used to monitor a

technical installation. The measurement documents are stored in the test equipment master record. The requirements for this functionality include the linkage of master inspection characteristics in the maintenance task list to measuring point master records by means of the class characteristics, as well as the creation of measuring point categories. Also required is the assignment of qualitative characteristics to the measuring point.

Q-9:   A. Define maintenance object and C. Define maintenance task list

A maintenance plan is the central planning object for a calibration inspection. Maintenance plan items control the maintenance and inspection tasks that are performed on maintenance objects. These items control when maintenance or inspection tasks are performed using maintenance cycles for which time and performance-based inspection intervals are defined. Depending on Customizing settings, as a maintenance plan is scheduled, maintenance calls are created and converted to orders when the calls are due. As an order is released, an inspection lot is created and the maintenance task list is selected and assigned to the maintenance plan. Following the selection and assignment of the task list, the calibration inspection operations are performed in chronological order and characteristic inspection results are recorded and valuated. Next, based on the valuation of the inspection characteristics, a usage decision for the inspection lot is documented and the inspection lot is completed. The completion of the calibration inspection triggers an update to the test equipment status in the equipment master record to reflect the test equipment valuation as indicated by the lot's usage decision. In turn, the activities of the calibration inspection are confirmed for the maintenance order using either the Results Recording or Inspection Lot Completion functions.

Q-10:   A. Provides the means to manage test equipment at the client level and C. Provides the means to document the maintenance history of test equipment

The Plant Maintenance component is used to create an equipment master record for each piece of test equipment. This master record provides the means to manage test equipment at the client level, document the equipment's maintenance history, as well as the equipment's status, which the calibration inspection determines. The equipment master record is also used to maintain static information about the equipment, such as the equipment's acquisition value and dimensions and the date the equipment was acquired. Also in the master record are the equipment's manufacturer, the work center and plant at which the equipment is located, and the equipment's serial number and cost center. The equipment's maintenance intervals, which are either time or performance-based, are also stored in the equipment master record.

Q-11:   A. Single-cycle plan and C. Multiple-counter plan

A maintenance plan is the central planning object for a calibration inspection. Items in the maintenance plan control the maintenance and inspection tasks that are performed on maintenance objects. These items use maintenance cycles for which time- and performance-based inspection intervals are defined to control when maintenance or inspection tasks are performed. To plan maintenance and inspection tasks on a performance basis, a single-cycle plan or multiple-counter plan can be used. Depending on Customizing settings, as a maintenance plan is scheduled, maintenance calls are created and converted to orders when the calls are due. As an order is released, an inspection lot is created and the maintenance task list is selected and assigned to the maintenance plan. Each task list structure contains operations and possibly sub-operations that describe the work to be performed during a calibration inspection. Inspection characteristics that describe what will be inspected using quantitative or qualitative inspection specifications can be assigned to the task list. Following the selection and assignment of the task list, the calibration inspection operations are performed in chronological order and characteristic inspection results are recorded and valuated. Next, based on the valuation of the inspection characteristics, a usage decision for the inspection lot is documented and the inspection lot is completed. The completion of the calibration inspection triggers an update to the test equipment status in the equipment master record to reflect the test equipment valuation as indicated by the lot's usage decision. In turn, the activities of the calibration inspection are confirmed for the maintenance order using either the Results Recording or Inspection Lot Completion functions.

Q-12:   A. Creation of inspection lot

A maintenance plan is the central planning object for a calibration inspection. Maintenance plan items control the maintenance and inspection tasks that are performed on maintenance objects. These items control when maintenance or inspection tasks are performed using maintenance cycles for which time and performance-based inspection intervals are defined. Depending on Customizing settings, as a maintenance plan is scheduled, maintenance calls are created and converted to orders when the calls are due. As an order is released, an inspection lot is created and the maintenance task list is selected and assigned to the maintenance plan. Each task list structure contains operations and possibly sub-operations that describe the work to be performed during a calibration inspection. Inspection characteristics that describe what will be inspected using quantitative or qualitative inspection specifications can be assigned to the task list. Following the selection and assignment of the task list, the calibration inspection operations are performed in chronological order and characteristic inspection results are recorded and valuated. Next, based on the valuation of the inspection characteristics, a usage decision for the inspection lot is documented and the inspection lot is completed. The completion of the calibration inspection triggers an update to the test equipment status in the equipment master record to reflect the test equipment valuation as indicated by the lot's usage decision. In turn, the activities of the calibration inspection are confirmed for the

maintenance order using either the Results Recording or Inspection Lot Completion functions.

Q-13:   A. Single-cycle plan

A maintenance plan is the central planning object for a calibration inspection. Items in the maintenance plan control the maintenance and inspection tasks that are performed on maintenance objects. These items use maintenance cycles for which time- and performance-based inspection intervals are defined to control when maintenance or inspection tasks are performed. A calibration inspection on a one-time basis, however, can be planned using a single-cycle plan. Depending on Customizing settings, as a maintenance plan is scheduled, maintenance calls are created and converted to orders when the calls are due. As an order is released, an inspection lot is created and the maintenance task list is selected and assigned to the maintenance plan.   Each task list structure contains operations and possibly sub-operations that describe the work to be performed during a calibration inspection. Inspection characteristics that describe what will be inspected using quantitative or qualitative inspection specifications can be assigned to the task list. Following the selection and assignment of the task list, the calibration inspection operations are performed in chronological order and characteristic inspection results are recorded and valuated. Next, based on the valuation of the inspection characteristics, a usage decision for the inspection lot is documented and the inspection lot is completed. The completion of the calibration inspection triggers an update to the test equipment status in the equipment master record to reflect the test equipment valuation as indicated by the lot's usage decision. In turn, the activities of the calibration inspection are confirmed for the maintenance order using either the Results Recording or Inspection Lot Completion functions.

Q-14:   A. The general maintenance task list is not linked to a maintenance object and B. The general maintenance task list serves as a proposal during the creation of maintenance order or maintenance task list

A maintenance plan is the central planning object for a calibration inspection. Maintenance plan items control the maintenance and inspection tasks that are performed on maintenance objects. These items control when maintenance or inspection tasks are performed using maintenance cycles for which time and performance-based inspection intervals are defined. Depending on Customizing settings, as a maintenance plan is scheduled, maintenance calls are created and converted to orders when the calls are due. As an order is released, an inspection lot is created and the maintenance task list – equipment, functional or general task list -- is selected and assigned to the maintenance plan. The general task list in particular is not linked to a maintenance object and can serve as a proposal during the creation of a maintenance order or task list. Each task list structure contains operations and possibly sub-operations that describe the work to be performed during a calibration inspection. Inspection characteristics that describe what will be inspected using quantitative or qualitative inspection specifications can be assigned to the task list. Following the selection and assignment of the task list, the calibration inspection operations are performed in chronological order and characteristic inspection results are recorded and valuated. Next, based on the valuation of the inspection characteristics, a usage decision for the inspection lot is documented and the inspection lot is completed. The completion of the calibration inspection triggers an update to the test equipment status in the equipment master record to reflect the test equipment valuation as indicated by the lot's usage decision. In turn, the activities of the calibration inspection are confirmed for the maintenance order using either the Results Recording or Inspection Lot Completion functions.

Q-15:   C. Maintenance order

The Controlling component uses orders to plan, monitor and settle operating costs. The maintenance order is the means by which activities that support calibration inspections are linked to cost assignment objects in the Controlling component. Like all costs accounted for by the Controlling component, calibration inspection costs are classified according to the functional origin of the cost by means of an order category. The functional origin of the costs is indicated by the order category 30. In turn, the order type is used to collect costs that originate with calibration inspection activities. Each inspection activity is recorded in terms of an activity type and activity times. The CO component then identifies the predefined price associated with the activity type. The CO component converts the activity time to an actual cost on the basis of a predefined price stored in the CO component. The costs are then settled to a cost object according to the account assignment that's entered when the order was created. During settlement, the actual costs incurred to conduct the inspection are allocated to one or more receivers. The system then automatically generates offsetting entries to the sender objects and the debit postings to the sender object remain in place.

Q-16:   A. Points at which inspection tasks are performed is determined by counter readings

A maintenance plan is the central planning object for a calibration inspection. Items in the plan control when and what maintenance and inspection tasks are performed on maintenance objects. The maintenance plan items also control the performance of the tasks with time- and performance-based inspection intervals, maintenance packages and scheduling parameters. The use of a performance-based maintenance plan ensures that counter readings determine the point at which inspection tasks are performed. Maintenance strategies, which define the inspection intervals, can be used with multiple maintenance plans. Different maintenance strategies with different inspection intervals can be defined for each inspection operation in a maintenance plan.

Q-17:   C. Schedule maintenance plan

A maintenance plan is the central planning object for a calibration inspection. Maintenance plan items control the maintenance and inspection tasks that are performed on maintenance objects. These items control when maintenance or inspection tasks are performed using maintenance cycles for which time and performance-based inspection intervals are defined. Depending on Customizing settings, as a maintenance plan is scheduled, maintenance calls are created on the basis of maintenance packages and scheduling parameters and converted to orders when the calls are due. As an order is released, an inspection lot is created and the maintenance task list is selected and assigned to the maintenance plan. Each task list structure contains operations and possibly sub-operations that describe the work to be performed during a calibration inspection. Inspection characteristics that describe what will be inspected using quantitative or qualitative inspection specifications can be assigned to the task list. Following the selection and assignment of the task list, the calibration inspection operations are performed in chronological order and characteristic inspection results are recorded and valuated. Next, based on the valuation of the inspection characteristics, a usage decision for the inspection lot is documented and the inspection lot is completed. The completion of the calibration inspection triggers an update to the test equipment status in the equipment master record to reflect the test equipment valuation as indicated by the lot's usage decision. In turn, the activities of the calibration inspection are confirmed for the maintenance order using either the Results Recording or Inspection Lot Completion functions.

Q-18:   A. Plant Maintenance – Maintenance Processing, B. Plant Maintenance – Preventive Maintenance and E. Quality Management Inspections

The planning, scheduling and processing of calibration inspections require the functions of the Test Equipment Management component, as well as those of the Technical Objects, Preventive Maintenance and Maintenance Processing Plant Maintenance components. Also required are functions of the Quality Planning and Quality Inspection Quality Management components, in addition to the functions of the Classification System.

Q-19:   B. Classification System

The planning, scheduling and processing of calibration inspections requires the functions of the Test Equipment Management component, as well as the functions of the Technical Objects, Preventive Maintenance and Maintenance Processing Plant Maintenance components. Also required are functions of the Quality Planning and Quality Inspection Quality Management components in addition to the Classification System.

Q-20:   A. Plant Maintenance

A maintenance plan, which is created using the Plant Maintenance component functionality, is the central planning object for a calibration inspection. Items in the maintenance plan control the maintenance and inspection tasks that are performed on maintenance objects. These items use maintenance cycles for which time- and performance-based inspection intervals are defined to control when maintenance or inspection tasks are performed. Depending on Customizing settings, as a maintenance plan is scheduled, maintenance calls are created and converted to orders when the calls are due. As an order is released, an inspection lot is created and the maintenance task list is selected and assigned to the maintenance plan. Each task list structure contains operations and possibly sub-operations that describe the work to be performed during a calibration inspection. Inspection characteristics that describe what will be inspected using quantitative or qualitative inspection specifications can be assigned to the task list. Following the selection and assignment of the task list, the calibration inspection operations are performed in chronological order and characteristic inspection results are recorded and valuated. Next, based on the valuation of the inspection characteristics, a usage decision for the inspection lot is documented and the inspection lot is completed. The completion of the calibration inspection triggers an update to the test equipment status in the equipment master record to reflect the test equipment valuation as indicated by the lot's usage decision. In turn, the activities of the calibration inspection are confirmed for the maintenance order using either the Results Recording or Inspection Lot Completion functions.

Q-21:   A. Change valuation mode

The quality of the items in an inspection lot can be evaluated on the basis of an inspection of samples, each of which can be selected by means of a sampling procedure. The two primary elements of a sampling procedure are the sampling type and the valuation mode. The sampling type controls the calculation of the sample size. In turn, the valuation mode specifies the rules that are used to determine if, following an inspection, a characteristic or sample is accepted or rejected for its intended purpose. The valuation rules are defined on the basis of the characteristic category and the sampling procedure that's assigned to the inspection characteristic. Examples of a valuation mode include the attributive inspection according to the number of nonconforming units, the variable inspection with a single-sided or double-sided tolerance range and the inspection without valuations parameters. If a characteristic is valuated on the wrong basis, the Change Valuation Mode function is used to select a different valuation mode.

Q-22:   A. Time-based maintenance plan with maintenance strategy, B. Performance-based maintenance plan with maintenance strategy, D. Time-based single cycle maintenance plan and E. Performance-based single cycle maintenance plan

A maintenance plan – time or performance based maintenance plan with a maintenance strategy, single-cycle time-based plan, single-cycle performance-based plan or multiple counter plan -- is the central planning object for a calibration inspection. Maintenance plan items control the maintenance and inspection tasks that are performed on maintenance objects. These items use maintenance cycles for which time- and/or performance-based inspection intervals are defined to control when maintenance or inspection tasks are performed. Depending on Customizing settings, as a maintenance plan is scheduled, maintenance calls are created and converted to orders when the calls are due. As an order is released, an inspection lot is created and the maintenance task list is selected and assigned to the maintenance plan. Each task list structure contains operations and possibly sub-operations that describe the work to be performed during a calibration inspection. Inspection characteristics that describe what will be inspected using quantitative or qualitative inspection specifications can be assigned to the task list. Following the selection and assignment of the task list, the calibration inspection operations are performed in chronological order and characteristic inspection results are recorded and valuated. Next, based on the valuation of the inspection characteristics, a usage decision for the inspection lot is documented and the inspection lot is completed. The completion of the calibration inspection triggers an update to the test equipment status in the equipment master record to reflect the test equipment valuation as indicated by the lot's usage decision. In turn, the activities of the calibration inspection are confirmed for the maintenance order using either the Results Recording or Inspection Lot Completion functions.

Q-23:   A. Operation and B. Sub-operation

A maintenance plan is the central planning object for a calibration inspection. Items in the maintenance plan control the maintenance and inspection tasks that are performed on maintenance objects. These items use maintenance cycles for which time- and performance-based inspection intervals are defined to control when maintenance or inspection tasks are performed.

Depending on Customizing settings, as a maintenance plan is scheduled, maintenance calls are created and converted to orders when the calls are due. As an order is released, an inspection lot is created and the maintenance task list is selected and assigned to the maintenance plan. Each task list structure contains operations and possibly sub-operations that describe the work to be performed during a calibration inspection. Inspection characteristics that describe what will be inspected using quantitative or qualitative inspection specifications can be assigned to the task list. Following the selection and assignment of the task list, the calibration inspection operations are performed in chronological order and characteristic inspection results are recorded and valuated. Next, based on the valuation of the inspection characteristics, a usage decision for the inspection lot is documented and the inspection lot is completed. The completion of the calibration inspection triggers an update to the test equipment status in the equipment master record to reflect the test equipment valuation as indicated by the lot's usage decision. In turn, the activities of the calibration inspection are confirmed for the maintenance order using either the Results Recording or Inspection Lot Completion functions.

Q-24:   A. Maintenance order

A maintenance plan is the central planning object for a calibration inspection. Maintenance plan items control the maintenance and inspection tasks that are performed on maintenance objects. These items control when maintenance or inspection tasks are

performed using maintenance cycles for which time and performance-based inspection intervals are defined. Depending on Customizing settings, as a maintenance plan is scheduled, maintenance calls are created and converted to orders when the calls are due. As an order is released, an inspection lot is created and the maintenance task list is selected and assigned to the maintenance plan. Each task list structure contains operations and possibly sub-operations that describe the work to be performed during a calibration inspection. The inspection activities are performed in the order in which they appear in the maintenance order. Inspection characteristics that describe what will be inspected using quantitative or qualitative inspection specifications can be assigned to the task list. Following the selection and assignment of the task list, the calibration inspection operations are performed in chronological order and characteristic inspection results are recorded and valuated. Next, based on the valuation of the inspection characteristics, a usage decision for the inspection lot is documented and the inspection lot is completed. The completion of the calibration inspection triggers an update to the test equipment status in the equipment master record to reflect the test equipment valuation as indicated by the lot's usage decision. In turn, the activities of the calibration inspection are confirmed for the maintenance order using either the Results Recording or Inspection Lot Completion functions.

Q-25:   C. Characteristic with selected set not assigned to measuring point

A usage decision code for an inspection lot concludes an inspection and documents its outcome. On the basis of this code and its linkage to follow-up functions, the functions can be executed automatically. One such follow-up action is the creation of measurement documents to record inspection results for each inspection point that's defined for the test equipment. The critical values obtained by measurement readings are recorded in the documents and used to monitor a technical installation. The measurement documents are stored in the test equipment master record. The requirements for this functionality include the linkage of master inspection characteristics in the maintenance task list to measuring point master records by means of the class characteristics, as well as the creation of measuring point categories. Also required is the assignment of qualitative characteristics to the measuring point.

Q-26:   B. Equipment master record and C. Task list

Test equipment is regularly inspected and calibrated to ensure it adheres to predefined performance criteria and is suitable for quality inspections. The results of the calibration inspection govern the release of the test equipment for subsequent use. The planning, scheduling and performance of calibration inspections require the master data, as well as the planning and processing functions of the Quality Management and Plant Maintenance components. For example, the inspection planning functions required to process a calibration inspection include creating equipment master records and test equipment groups, linking master inspection characteristics to class characteristics using the classification system and defining inspection specifications for both quantitative and qualitative characteristics. Additional planning functions include creating inspection characteristics for the maintenance task list operations and maintenance cycles in the maintenance plan, monitoring maintenance schedules and the status of the test equipment, and creating and releasing maintenance orders. In turn, the inspection processing functions include documenting inspection results for each piece of test equipment and creating maintenance notifications. valuating test equipment in an inspection lot, entering the usage decision for the inspection lot and confirming services for maintenance orders. Additional processing functions include conducting follow-up actions for an inspection lot usage decision and updating the Plant Maintenance and Quality Management Information Systems.

Q-27:   A. Equipment usage and B. Time schedule

The Plant Maintenance component is used to create an equipment master record for each piece of test equipment. This master record provides the means to manage test equipment at the client level, document the equipment's maintenance history, as well as the equipment's status, which the calibration inspection determines. The equipment master record is also used to maintain static information about the equipment, such as the equipment's acquisition value and dimensions and the date the equipment was acquired. Also in the master record are the equipment's manufacturer, the work center and plant at which the equipment is located, and the equipment's serial number and cost center. The equipment's maintenance intervals, which are either time or performance-based, are also stored in the equipment master record.

Q-28:   A. Measuring point categories and C. Assignment of class characteristics with unit of measure to measuring points

A usage decision code for an inspection lot concludes an inspection and documents its outcome. On the basis of this code and its linkage to follow-up functions, the functions can be executed automatically. One such follow-up action is the creation of measurement documents to record inspection results for each inspection point that's defined for the test equipment. The critical values obtained by measurement readings are recorded in the documents and used to monitor a technical installation. The measurement documents are stored in the test equipment master record. The requirements for this functionality include the linkage of master inspection characteristics in the maintenance task list to measuring point master records by means of the class characteristics, as well as the creation of measuring point categories. Also required is the assignment of qualitative characteristics to the measuring point.

Q-29:   A. Equipment task list and B. General task list

A maintenance plan is the central planning object for a calibration inspection. Maintenance plan items control the maintenance and inspection tasks that are performed on maintenance objects. These items control when maintenance or inspection tasks are performed using maintenance cycles for which time and performance-based inspection intervals are defined. Depending on Customizing settings, as a maintenance plan is scheduled, maintenance calls are created and converted to orders when the calls are due. As an order is released, an inspection lot is created and the maintenance task list – equipment, general or functional task list -- is selected and assigned to the maintenance plan. Each task list structure contains operations and possibly sub-operations that describe the work to be performed during a calibration inspection. Inspection characteristics that describe what will be inspected using quantitative or qualitative inspection specifications can be assigned to the task list. Following the selection and assignment of the task list, the calibration inspection operations are performed in chronological order and characteristic inspection results are recorded and valuated. Next, based on the valuation of the inspection characteristics, a usage decision for the inspection lot is documented and the inspection lot is completed. The completion of the calibration inspection triggers an update to the test equipment status in the equipment master record to reflect the test equipment valuation as indicated by the lot's usage decision. In turn, the activities of the calibration inspection are confirmed for the maintenance order using either the Results Recording or Inspection Lot Completion functions.

Q-30:   A. Plaint Maintenance

A maintenance plan is the central planning object for a calibration inspection. Maintenance plan items control

the maintenance and inspection tasks that are performed on maintenance objects. These items control when maintenance or inspection tasks are performed using maintenance cycles for which time and performance-based inspection intervals are defined. Depending on Customizing settings, as a maintenance plan is scheduled, maintenance calls are created and converted to orders when the calls are due. As an order is released, an inspection lot is created and the maintenance task list is selected and assigned to the maintenance plan. Each task list structure contains operations and possibly sub-operations that describe the work to be performed during a calibration inspection. Inspection characteristics that describe what will be inspected using quantitative or qualitative inspection specifications can be assigned to the task list. Following the selection and assignment of the task list, the calibration inspection operations are performed in chronological order and characteristic inspection results are recorded and valuated. Next, based on the valuation of the inspection characteristics, a usage decision for the inspection lot is documented and the inspection lot is completed. The completion of the calibration inspection triggers an update to the test equipment status in the equipment master record to reflect the test equipment valuation as indicated by the lot's usage decision. In turn, the activities of the calibration inspection are confirmed for the maintenance order using the Plant Maintenance component.

Q-31:   A. Maintenance plan

A maintenance plan is the central planning object for a calibration inspection. Maintenance plan items control the maintenance and inspection tasks that are performed on maintenance objects. These items control when maintenance or inspection tasks are performed using maintenance cycles for which time and performance-based inspection intervals are defined. Depending on Customizing settings, as a maintenance plan is scheduled, maintenance calls are created and converted to orders when the calls are due. As an order is released, an inspection lot is created and the maintenance task list – equipment, functional or general task list -- is selected and assigned to the maintenance plan. Each task list structure contains operations and possibly sub-operations that describe the work to be performed during a calibration inspection. Inspection characteristics that describe what will be inspected using quantitative or qualitative inspection specifications can be assigned to the task list. Following the selection and assignment of the task list, the calibration inspection operations are performed in chronological order and characteristic inspection results are recorded and valuated. Next, based on the valuation of the inspection characteristics, a usage decision for the inspection lot is documented and the inspection lot is completed. The completion of the calibration inspection triggers an update to the test equipment status in the equipment master record to reflect the test equipment valuation as indicated by the lot's usage decision. In turn, the activities of the calibration inspection are confirmed for the maintenance order.

Q-32:   B. Maintenance task list

A maintenance plan is the central planning object for a calibration inspection. Maintenance plan items control the maintenance and inspection tasks that are performed on maintenance objects. These items control when maintenance or inspection tasks are performed using maintenance cycles for which time and performance-based inspection intervals are defined. Depending on Customizing settings, as a maintenance plan is scheduled, maintenance calls are created and converted to orders when the calls are due. As an order is released, an inspection lot is created and the maintenance task list is selected and assigned to the maintenance plan. 33Each task list structure contains operations and possibly sub-operations that describe the work to be performed during a calibration inspection. Inspection characteristics that describe what will be inspected using quantitative or qualitative inspection specifications can be assigned to the task list. Following the selection and assignment of the task list, the calibration inspection operations are performed in chronological order and characteristic inspection results are recorded and valuated. Next, based on the valuation of the inspection characteristics, a usage decision for the inspection lot is documented and the inspection lot is completed. The completion of the calibration inspection triggers an update to the test equipment status in the equipment master record to reflect the test equipment valuation as indicated by the lot's usage decision. In turn, the activities of the calibration inspection are confirmed for the maintenance order using the Plant Maintenance component.

Q-33:   A. QM Test Equipment Management

The planning, scheduling and processing of calibration inspections require the functions of the Test Equipment Management component, as well as those of the Technical Objects, Preventive Maintenance and Maintenance Processing Plant Maintenance components. Also required are functions of the Quality Planning and Quality Inspection Quality Management components, in addition to the functions of the Classification System.

Q-34:   C. Equipment master record

The Plant Maintenance component is used to create an equipment master record for each piece of test equipment. This master record provides the means to manage test equipment at the client level, document the equipment's maintenance history, as well as the equipment's status, which the calibration inspection determines. The equipment master record is also used to maintain static information about the equipment, such as the equipment's acquisition value and dimensions and the date the equipment was acquired. Also in the master record are the equipment's manufacturer, the work center and plant at which the equipment is located, and the equipment's serial number and cost center. The equipment's maintenance intervals, which are either time or performance-based, are also stored in the equipment master record.

Q-35:   B. Linkage of the master inspection characteristic to class characteristic in the classification system

A usage decision code for an inspection lot concludes an inspection and documents its outcome. On the basis of this code and its linkage to follow-up functions, the functions can be executed automatically. One such follow-up action is the creation of measurement documents to record inspection results for each inspection point that's defined for the test equipment. The critical values obtained by measurement readings are recorded in the documents and used to monitor a technical installation. The measurement documents are stored in the test equipment master record. The requirements for this functionality include the linkage of master inspection characteristics in the maintenance task list to measuring point master records by means of the class characteristics, as well as the creation of measuring point categories. Also required is the assignment of qualitative characteristics to the measuring point.

Q-36:   A. Activities of the planning phase of a calibration inspection

Test equipment is regularly inspected and calibrated to ensure it adheres to predefined performance criteria and is suitable for quality inspections. The results of the calibration inspection govern the release of the test equipment for subsequent use. The planning, scheduling and performance of calibration inspections require the master data, as well as the planning and processing functions of the Quality Management and Plant Maintenance components. For example, the inspection planning functions required to process a calibration inspection include creating equipment master records and test equipment groups, linking master inspection characteristics to class characteristics using the classification system and defining inspection specifications for both quantitative and qualitative characteristics. Additional planning functions include creating inspection characteristics for the maintenance task list operations and maintenance cycles in the maintenance plan, monitoring maintenance schedules and the status of the test equipment, and creating and releasing maintenance orders. In turn, the inspection processing functions include documenting inspection results for each piece of test equipment and creating maintenance notifications. valuating test equipment in an inspection lot, entering the usage decision for the inspection lot and confirming services for maintenance orders. Additional processing functions include conducting follow-up actions for an inspection lot usage decision, and updating the Plant Maintenance and Quality Management Information System.

Q-37:   C. Maintenance plan

A maintenance plan is the central planning object for a calibration inspection. Maintenance plan items control the maintenance and inspection tasks that are performed on maintenance objects. These items control when maintenance or inspection tasks are performed using maintenance cycles for which time and performance-based inspection intervals are defined.

Depending on Customizing settings, as a maintenance plan is scheduled, maintenance calls are created and converted to orders when the calls are due. As an order is released, an inspection lot is created and the maintenance task list – equipment, functional or general task list -- is selected and assigned to the maintenance plan. Each task list structure contains operations and possibly sub-operations that describe the work to be performed during a calibration inspection. Inspection characteristics that describe what will be inspected using quantitative or qualitative inspection specifications can be assigned to the task list. Following the selection and assignment of the task list, the calibration inspection operations are performed in chronological order and characteristic inspection results are recorded and valuated. Next, based on the valuation of the inspection characteristics, a usage decision for the inspection lot is documented and the inspection lot is completed. The completion of the calibration inspection triggers an update to the test equipment status in the equipment master record to reflect the test equipment valuation as indicated by the lot's usage decision. In turn, the activities of the calibration inspection are confirmed for the maintenance order.

Q-38:   A. May consist of operations and sub-operations, B. May be an equipment, functional location or general maintenance task list and D. The operation can be performed by internal or external partner

A maintenance plan is the central planning object for a calibration inspection. Maintenance plan items control

the maintenance and inspection tasks that are performed on maintenance objects. These items control when maintenance or inspection tasks are performed using maintenance cycles for which time and performance-based inspection intervals are defined. Depending on Customizing settings, as a maintenance plan is scheduled, maintenance calls are created and converted to orders when the calls are due. As an order is released, an inspection lot is created and the maintenance task list is selected and assigned to the maintenance plan. Each task list structure contains operations and possibly sub-operations that describe the work to be performed by internal or external partners during a calibration inspection. Inspection characteristics that describe what will be inspected using quantitative or qualitative inspection specifications can be assigned to the task list. Following the selection and assignment of the task list, the calibration inspection operations are performed in chronological order and characteristic inspection results are recorded and valuated. Next, based on the valuation of the inspection characteristics, a usage decision for the inspection lot is documented and the inspection lot is completed. The completion of the calibration inspection triggers an update to the test equipment status in the equipment master record to reflect the test equipment valuation as indicated by the lot's usage decision. In turn, the activities of the calibration inspection are confirmed for the maintenance order.

Q-39:   B. Plan maintenance work to be performed at a particular work center and C. Settle costs of test equipment maintenance

The Controlling component uses orders to plan, monitor and settle operating costs. The maintenance order is the means by which activities that support calibration inspections are linked to cost assignment objects in the Controlling component. Like all costs accounted for by the Controlling component, test equipment maintenance costs are classified according to the functional origin of the cost by means of an order category. The functional origin of the costs is indicated by the order category 30. In turn, the 14 order type is used to collect costs that originate with calibration inspection activities. Each inspection activity is recorded in terms of an activity type and activity times. The CO component then identifies the predefined price associated with the activity type. The CO component converts the activity time to an actual cost on the basis of the predefined price stored in the CO component. The calibration inspection costs are then settled to a cost object according to the account assignment that's entered when the order was created. During settlement, the actual costs incurred to conduct the inspection are allocated to one or more receivers. The system then automatically generates offsetting entries to the sender objects and the debit postings to the sender object remain in place.

Q-40:   A. Creation and release of maintenance order

A maintenance plan is the central planning object for a calibration inspection. Maintenance plan items control the maintenance and inspection tasks that are performed on maintenance objects. These items control when maintenance or inspection tasks are

performed using maintenance cycles for which time and performance-based inspection intervals are defined. Depending on Customizing settings, as a maintenance plan is scheduled, maintenance calls are created and converted to orders when the calls are due. As an order is released, an inspection lot is created and the maintenance task list is selected and assigned to the maintenance plan. Each task list structure contains operations and possibly sub-operations that describe the work to be performed during a calibration inspection. Inspection characteristics that describe what will be inspected using quantitative or qualitative inspection specifications can be assigned to the task list. Following the selection and assignment of the task list, the calibration inspection operations are performed in chronological order and characteristic inspection results are recorded and valuated. Next, based on the valuation of the inspection characteristics, a usage decision for the inspection lot is documented and the inspection lot is completed. The completion of the calibration inspection triggers an update to the test equipment status in the equipment master record to reflect the test equipment valuation as indicated by the lot's usage decision. In turn, the activities of the calibration inspection are confirmed for the maintenance order.

Q-41:   A. Inspection type and C. Order type

Test equipment is regularly inspected and calibrated to ensure that it adheres to predefined performance criteria is suitable for quality inspections. The results of the calibration inspection govern the release of the test equipment for subsequent use. The planning, scheduling and performance of calibration inspections require the master data, as well as the planning and processing functions of the Test Equipment Management component. In particular, the functions required to plan a calibration inspection include the creation of an equipment master record, measuring points with reference to class characteristics and a maintenance strategy. Also required are the creation of a task list, an inspection lot, master inspection characteristics and a maintenance plan. In turn, Customizing requirements include the definition of an inspection type, inspection points, default values for the inspection type and an order type. Also required are the assignment of inspection types to the order types, materials to task list operations, objects to the maintenance plan items and master inspection characteristics to operations.

Q-42:   A. Record inspection results for measuring points of test equipment using measurement documents

A usage decision code for an inspection lot concludes an inspection and documents its outcome. On the basis of this code and its linkage to follow-up functions, the functions can be executed automatically. One such follow-up action is the creation of measurement documents to record inspection results for each inspection point that's defined for the test equipment. The critical values obtained by measurement readings are recorded in the documents and used to monitor a technical installation. The measurement documents are stored in the test equipment master record. The requirements for this functionality include the linkage of master inspection characteristics in the maintenance task list to measuring point master records by means of the class characteristics, as well as the creation of measuring point categories. Also required is the assignment of qualitative characteristics to the measuring point.

Q-43:   C. Define inspection points

Test equipment is regularly inspected and calibrated to ensure that it adheres to predefined performance criteria is suitable for quality inspections. The results of the calibration inspection govern the release of the test equipment for subsequent use. The planning, scheduling and performance of calibration inspections require the master data, as well as the planning and processing functions of the Test Equipment Management component. In particular, the functions required to plan a calibration inspection include the creation of an equipment master record, measuring points with reference to class characteristics and a maintenance strategy. Also required are the creation of a task list, an inspection lot, master inspection characteristics and a maintenance plan. In turn, Customizing requirements include the definition of an inspection type, inspection points, default values for the inspection type and an order type. Also required are the assignment of inspection types to the order types, materials to task list operations, objects to the maintenance plan items and master inspection characteristics to operations.

Q-44:   A. Test Equipment Management: Create
Measuring Point for Equipment and B. Test Equipment
Management: Edit Equipment Master Record

A usage decision code for an inspection lot concludes
an inspection and documents its outcome. On the
basis of this code and its linkage to follow-up functions,
the functions can be executed automatically. One such
follow-up action is the creation of measurement
documents to record inspection results for each
inspection point that's defined for the test equipment.
The critical values obtained by measurement readings
are recorded in the documents and used to monitor a
technical installation. The measurement documents are
stored in the test equipment master record. The
requirements for this functionality include the linkage
of master inspection characteristics in the maintenance
task list to measuring point master records by means of
the class characteristics, as well as the creation of
measuring point categories. Also required is the
assignment of qualitative characteristics to the
measuring point.

Q-45:   C. Link master inspection characteristics to
class characteristics using the classification system and
D. Define inspection specifications for both
quantitative and qualitative characteristics

Test equipment is regularly inspected and calibrated to
ensure that it adheres to predefined performance
criteria is suitable for quality inspections. The results of
the calibration inspection govern the release of the test
equipment for subsequent use.   The planning,

scheduling and performance of calibration inspections require the master data, as well as the planning and processing functions of the Test Equipment Management component. In particular, the functions required to plan a calibration inspection include the creation of an equipment master record, measuring points with reference to class characteristics and a maintenance strategy. Also required are the creation of a task list, an inspection lot, master inspection characteristics and a maintenance plan. In turn, Customizing requirements include the definition of an inspection type, inspection points, default values for the inspection type and an order type. Also required are the assignment of inspection types to the order types, materials to task list operations, objects to the maintenance plan items and master inspection characteristics to operations.

Q-46:   A. Create Maintenance Task List and B. Create Test Equipment Master Record

Test equipment is regularly inspected and calibrated to ensure that it adheres to predefined performance criteria is suitable for quality inspections. The results of the calibration inspection govern the release of the test equipment for subsequent use. The planning, scheduling and performance of calibration inspections require the master data, as well as the planning and processing functions of the Test Equipment Management component. In particular, the functions required to plan a calibration inspection include the creation of an equipment master record, measuring points with reference to class characteristics and a

maintenance strategy. Also required are the creation of a task list, an inspection lot, master inspection characteristics and a maintenance plan. In turn, Customizing requirements include the definition of an inspection type, inspection points, default values for the inspection typ
e and an order type. Also required are the assignment of inspection types to the order types, materials to task list operations, objects to the maintenance plan items and master inspection characteristics to operations.

Q-47:   A. Usage Decision

A maintenance plan is the central planning object for a calibration inspection. Maintenance plan items control the maintenance and inspection tasks that are performed on maintenance objects. These items control when maintenance or inspection tasks are performed using maintenance cycles for which time and performance-based inspection intervals are defined. Depending on Customizing settings, as a maintenance plan is scheduled, maintenance calls are created and converted to orders when the calls are due. As an order is released, an inspection lot is created and the maintenance task list – equipment, functional or general task list -- is selected and assigned to the maintenance plan. Each task list structure contains operations and possibly sub-operations that describe the work to be performed during a calibration inspection. Inspection characteristics that describe what will be inspected using quantitative or qualitative inspection specifications can be assigned to the task list. Following the selection and assignment of the task list, the calibration inspection operations are performed in chronological order and characteristic inspection results are recorded and valuated. Next, based on the valuation of the inspection characteristics, a usage decision for the inspection lot is documented and the inspection lot is completed. The completion of the calibration inspection triggers an update to the test equipment status in the equipment master record to reflect the test equipment valuation as indicated by the lot's usage decision. In turn, the activities of the calibration inspection are confirmed for the maintenance order using either the Results Recording or Inspection Lot Completion functions.

Q-48:   A. Create measuring point for equipment and B. Edit equipment master record

A usage decision code for an inspection lot concludes an inspection and documents its outcome. On the basis of this code and its linkage to follow-up functions, the functions can be executed automatically. One such follow-up action is the creation of measurement documents to record inspection results for each inspection point that's defined for the test equipment. The critical values obtained by measurement readings are recorded in the documents and used to monitor a technical installation. The measurement documents are stored in the test equipment master record. The requirements for this functionality include the linkage of master inspection characteristics in the maintenance task list to measuring point master records by means of the class characteristics, as well as the creation of measuring point categories. Also required is the assignment of qualitative characteristics to the measuring point.

Q-49:   B. Equipment task list and C. Functional location task list

A maintenance plan is the central planning object for a calibration inspection. Maintenance plan items control the maintenance and inspection tasks that are performed on maintenance objects. These items control when maintenance or inspection tasks are performed using maintenance cycles for which time and performance-based inspection intervals are defined. Depending on Customizing settings, as a maintenance plan is scheduled, maintenance calls are created and converted to orders when the calls are due. As an order is released, an inspection lot is created and the maintenance task list -- equipment, functional or general task list -- is selected and assigned to the maintenance plan. Each task list structure contains operations and possibly sub-operations that describe the work to be performed during a calibration inspection. Inspection characteristics that describe what will be inspected using quantitative or qualitative inspection specifications can be assigned to the task list. Following the selection and assignment of the task list, the calibration inspection operations are performed in chronological order and characteristic inspection results are recorded and valuated. Next, based on the valuation of the inspection characteristics, a usage decision for the inspection lot is documented and the inspection lot is completed. The completion of the calibration inspection triggers an update to the test equipment status in the equipment master record to reflect the test equipment valuation as indicated by the lot's usage decision. In turn, the activities of the calibration inspection are confirmed for the maintenance order.

Q-50: A. Maintenance order

A maintenance plan is the central planning object for a calibration inspection. Maintenance plan items control the maintenance and inspection tasks that are performed on maintenance objects. These items control when maintenance or inspection tasks are performed using maintenance cycles for which time and performance-based inspection intervals are defined. Depending on Customizing settings, as a maintenance plan is scheduled, maintenance calls are created and then converted to orders that determine where an inspection will be performed when the calls are due. As an order is released, an inspection lot is created and the maintenance task list is selected and assigned to the maintenance plan. Each task list structure contains operations and possibly sub-operations that describe the work to be performed during a calibration inspection. Inspection characteristics that describe what will be inspected using quantitative or qualitative inspection specifications can be assigned to the task list. Following the selection and assignment of the task list, the calibration inspection operations are performed in chronological order and characteristic inspection results are recorded and valuated. Next, based on the valuation of the inspection characteristics, a usage decision for the inspection lot is documented and the inspection lot is completed. The completion of the calibration inspection triggers an update to the test equipment status in the equipment master record to

reflect the test equipment valuation as indicated by the lot's usage decision. In turn, the activities of the calibration inspection are confirmed for the maintenance order.

Q-51:   A. Resource

A maintenance plan is the central planning object for a calibration inspection. Maintenance plan items control the maintenance and inspection tasks that are performed on maintenance objects. These items control when maintenance or inspection tasks are performed using maintenance cycles for which time and performance-based inspection intervals are defined. Depending on Customizing settings, as a maintenance plan is scheduled, maintenance calls are created and then converted to orders, which refer to required resources, when the calls are due. As an order is released, an inspection lot is created and the maintenance task list is selected and assigned to the maintenance plan. Each task list structure contains operations and possibly sub-operations that describe the work to be performed and the resources to be used during a calibration inspection. Inspection characteristics that describe what will be inspected using quantitative or qualitative inspection specifications can be assigned to the task list. Following the selection and assignment of the task list, the calibration inspection operations are performed in chronological order and characteristic inspection results are recorded and valuated. Next, based on the valuation of the inspection characteristics, a usage decision for the inspection lot is documented and the inspection lot is completed. The

156

completion of the calibration inspection triggers an update to the test equipment status in the equipment master record to reflect the test equipment valuation as indicated by the lot's usage decision. In turn, the activities of the calibration inspection are confirmed for the maintenance order using either the Results Recording or Inspection Lot Completion functions.

Q-52:   B. Maintenance task list

A maintenance plan is the central planning object for a calibration inspection. Maintenance plan items control the maintenance and inspection tasks that are performed on maintenance objects. These items control when maintenance or inspection tasks are performed using maintenance cycles for which time and performance-based inspection intervals are defined. Depending on Customizing settings, as a maintenance plan is scheduled, maintenance calls are created and converted to orders when the calls are due. As an order is released, an inspection lot is created and the maintenance task list is selected and assigned to the maintenance plan. Each task list structure contains operations and possibly sub-operations that describe the work steps to be performed during a calibration inspection. Inspection characteristics that describe what will be inspected using quantitative or qualitative inspection specifications can be assigned to the task list. Following the selection and assignment of the task list, the calibration inspection operations are performed in chronological order and characteristic inspection results are recorded and valuated. Next, based on the valuation of the inspection characteristics, a usage

decision for the inspection lot is documented and the inspection lot is completed. The completion of the calibration inspection triggers an update to the test equipment status in the equipment master record to reflect the test equipment valuation as indicated by the lot's usage decision. In turn, the activities of the calibration inspection are confirmed for the maintenance order.

Q-53:   B. Enter equipment key and C. Enter test equipment category

The Plant Maintenance component is used to create an equipment master record for each piece of test equipment. This master record provides the means to manage test equipment at the client level, document the equipment's maintenance history, as well as the equipment's status, which the calibration inspection determines. The equipment master record is also used to maintain static information about the equipment, such as the equipment's acquisition value and dimensions and the date the equipment was acquired. Also in the master record are the equipment's manufacturer, the work center and plant at which the equipment is located, and the equipment's serial number and cost center. The equipment's maintenance intervals, which are either time or performance-based, are also stored in the equipment master record.

Q-54:   A. Class characteristic is assigned to the master inspection characteristic and measuring point/counter and B. Master inspection characteristics

A usage decision code for an inspection lot concludes an inspection and documents its outcome. On the basis of this code and its linkage to follow-up functions, the functions can be executed automatically. One such follow-up action is the creation of measurement documents to record inspection results for each inspection point that's defined for the test equipment. The critical values obtained by measurement readings are recorded in the documents and used to monitor a technical installation. The measurement documents are stored in the test equipment master record. The requirements for this functionality include the linkage of master inspection characteristics in the maintenance task list to measuring point master records by means of the class characteristics, as well as the creation of measuring point categories. Also required is the assignment of qualitative characteristics to the measuring point.

Q-55:   B. Inspection can be conducted

A maintenance plan is the central planning object for a calibration inspection. Maintenance plan items control the maintenance and inspection tasks that are performed on maintenance objects. These items control when maintenance or inspection tasks are performed using maintenance cycles for which time and performance-based inspection intervals are defined. Depending on Customizing settings, as a maintenance plan is scheduled, maintenance calls are created and converted to orders when the calls are due. As an order is released, an inspection lot is created and the maintenance task list is selected and assigned to the maintenance plan. Each task list structure contains

operations and possibly sub-operations that describe the work to be performed during a calibration inspection. Inspection characteristics that describe what will be inspected using quantitative or qualitative inspection specifications can be assigned to the task list. Following the selection and assignment of the task list, the calibration inspection operations are performed in chronological order and characteristic inspection results are recorded and valuated. Next, based on the valuation of the inspection characteristics, a usage decision for the inspection lot is documented and the inspection lot is completed. The completion of the calibration inspection triggers an update to the test equipment status in the equipment master record to reflect the test equipment valuation as indicated by the lot's usage decision. In turn, the activities of the calibration inspection are confirmed for the maintenance order.

Q-56: C. Define task list, D. Link master inspection characteristics to inspection characteristics in the classification system and E. Define maintenance strategy

Test equipment is regularly inspected and calibrated to ensure that it adheres to predefined performance criteria is suitable for quality inspections. The results of the calibration inspection govern the release of the test equipment for subsequent use. The planning, scheduling and performance of calibration inspections require the master data, as well as the planning and processing functions of the Test Equipment Management component. In particular, the functions required to plan a calibration inspection include the creation of an equipment master record, measuring points with reference to class characteristics and a maintenance strategy. Also required are the creation of a task list, an inspection lot, master inspection characteristics and a maintenance plan. In turn, Customizing requirements include the definition of an inspection type, inspection points, default values for the inspection type and an order type. Also required are the assignment of inspection types to the order types, materials to task list operations, objects to the maintenance plan items and master inspection characteristics to operations.

Q-57:   B. Define inspection type and C. Define order type

Test equipment is regularly inspected and calibrated to ensure that it adheres to predefined performance criteria is suitable for quality inspections. The results of the calibration inspection govern the release of the test equipment for subsequent use. The planning, scheduling and performance of calibration inspections require the master data, as well as the planning and processing functions of the Test Equipment Management component. In particular, the functions required to plan a calibration inspection include the creation of an equipment master record, measuring points with reference to class characteristics and a maintenance strategy. Also required are the creation of a task list, an inspection lot, master inspection characteristics and a maintenance plan. In turn, Customizing requirements include the definition of an inspection type, inspection points, default values for the inspection type and an order type. Also required are the assignment of inspection types to the order types, materials to task list operations, objects to the maintenance plan items and master inspection characteristics to operations.

Q-58:   B. Assign class characteristic to measuring point

A usage decision code for an inspection lot concludes an inspection and documents its outcome. On the basis of this code and its linkage to follow-up functions, the functions can be executed automatically. One such follow-up action is the creation of measurement documents to record inspection results for each inspection point that's defined for the test equipment. The critical values obtained by measurement readings are recorded in the documents and used to monitor a technical installation. The measurement documents are stored in the test equipment master record. The requirements for this functionality include the linkage of master inspection characteristics in the maintenance task list to measuring point master records by means of the class characteristics, as well as the creation of measuring point categories. Also required is the assignment of qualitative characteristics to the measuring point.

Q-59:   A. Plant Maintenance

The Plant Maintenance component is used to create an equipment master record for each piece of test equipment. This master record provides the means to manage test equipment at the client level, document the equipment's maintenance history, as well as the equipment's status, which the calibration inspection determines. The equipment master record is also used to maintain static information about the equipment, such as the equipment's acquisition value and dimensions and the date the equipment was acquired. Also in the master record are the equipment's manufacturer, the work center and plant at which the equipment is located, and the equipment's serial number and cost center. The equipment's maintenance intervals, which are either time or performance-based, are also stored in the equipment master record.

Q-60:   A. Plant Maintenance Information System and B. Quality Management Information System

The Plant Maintenance and Quality Management Information Systems are the primary databases for the Plant Maintenance and Quality Management solutions. These systems can be updated with data generated by the Test Equipment Management component. These information systems collect the PM and QM data from within an organization that enables the user to analyze individual operational areas including test equipment maintenance. The creation of the evaluations, which are generated according to Customizing settings, can be scheduled for particular dates.

Q-61:   B. Maintenance task list

A maintenance plan is the central planning object for a calibration inspection. Maintenance plan items control the maintenance and inspection tasks that are performed on maintenance objects. These items control when maintenance or inspection tasks are performed using maintenance cycles for which time and performance-based inspection intervals are defined. Depending on Customizing settings, as a maintenance plan is scheduled, maintenance calls are created and converted to orders when the calls are due. As an order is released, an inspection lot is created and the maintenance task list is selected and assigned to the maintenance plan. Each task list structure contains operations and possibly sub-operations that describe the tasks to be performed during a calibration inspection. Inspection characteristics that describe what will be inspected using quantitative or qualitative inspection specifications can be assigned to the task list. Following the selection and assignment of the task list, the calibration inspection operations are performed in chronological order and characteristic inspection results are recorded and valuated. Next, based on the valuation of the inspection characteristics, a usage decision for the inspection lot is documented and the inspection lot is completed. The completion of the calibration inspection triggers an update to the test equipment status in the equipment master record to reflect the test equipment valuation as indicated by the lot's usage decision. In turn, the activities of the calibration inspection are confirmed for the maintenance order.

Q-62: A. Tasks of maintenance task list are scheduled on a calendar basis

A maintenance plan is the central planning object for a calibration inspection. Maintenance plan items control the maintenance and inspection tasks that are performed on maintenance objects. These items control when maintenance or inspection tasks are performed using maintenance cycles for which time and performance-based inspection intervals are defined. Depending on Customizing settings, as a maintenance plan is scheduled, maintenance calls are created and converted to orders when the calls are due. As an order is released, an inspection lot is created and the maintenance task list is selected and assigned to the maintenance plan. Each task list structure contains operations and possibly sub-operations that describe the work to be performed during a calibration inspection. Inspection characteristics that describe what will be inspected using quantitative or qualitative inspection specifications can be assigned to the task list. Following the selection and assignment of the task list, the calibration inspection operations are performed in chronological order and characteristic inspection results are recorded and valuated. Next, based on the valuation of the inspection characteristics, a usage decision for the inspection lot is documented and the inspection lot is completed. The completion of the calibration inspection triggers an update to the test equipment status in the equipment master record to reflect the test equipment valuation as indicated by the lot's usage decision. In turn, the activities of the calibration inspection are confirmed for the

maintenance order using either the Results Recording or Inspection Lot Completion functions.

Q-63:   A. Inspection type and B. Inspection points

Test equipment is regularly inspected and calibrated to ensure that it adheres to predefined performance criteria is suitable for quality inspections. The results of the calibration inspection govern the release of the test equipment for subsequent use. The planning, scheduling and performance of calibration inspections require the master data, as well as the planning and processing functions of the Test Equipment Management component. In particular, the functions required to plan a calibration inspection include the creation of an equipment master record, measuring points with reference to class characteristics and a maintenance strategy. Also required are the creation of a task list, an inspection lot, master inspection characteristics and a maintenance plan. In turn, Customizing requirements include the definition of an inspection type, inspection points, default values for the inspection type and an order type. Also required are the assignment of inspection types to the order types, materials to task list operations, objects to the maintenance plan items and master inspection characteristics to operations.

Q-64:   C. Maintenance order

A maintenance plan is the central planning object for a calibration inspection. Maintenance plan items control the maintenance and inspection tasks that are

performed on maintenance objects. These items control when maintenance or inspection tasks are performed using maintenance cycles for which time and performance-based inspection intervals are defined. Depending on Customizing settings, as a maintenance plan is scheduled, maintenance calls are created and converted to orders when the calls are due. As the order that defines activities to be performed at a work station is released, an inspection lot is created and the maintenance task list, which determines the maintenance activities to be performed, is selected and assigned to the maintenance plan. Each task list structure contains operations and possibly sub-operations that describe the work to be performed during a calibration inspection. Inspection characteristics that describe what will be inspected using quantitative or qualitative inspection specifications can be assigned to the task list. Following the selection and assignment of the task list, the calibration inspection operations are performed in chronological order and characteristic inspection results are recorded and valuated. Next, based on the valuation of the inspection characteristics, a usage decision for the inspection lot is documented and the inspection lot is completed. The completion of the calibration inspection triggers an update to the test equipment status in the equipment master record to reflect the test equipment valuation as indicated by the lot's usage decision. In turn, the activities of the calibration inspection are confirmed for the maintenance order.

Q-65:   A. Assignment of task list to maintenance plan
and B. Assignment of inspection characteristics to
operations

Test equipment is regularly inspected and calibrated to
ensure that it adheres to predefined performance
criteria is suitable for quality inspections. The results of
the calibration inspection govern the release of the test
equipment for subsequent use. The planning,
scheduling and performance of calibration inspections
require the master data, as well as the planning and
processing functions of the Test Equipment
Management component. In particular, the functions
required to plan a calibration inspection include the
creation of an equipment master record, measuring
points with reference to class characteristics and a
maintenance strategy. Also required are the creation of
a task list, an inspection lot, master inspection
characteristics and a maintenance plan. In turn,
Customizing requirements include the definition of an
inspection type, inspection points, default values for the
inspection type and an order type. Also required are
the assignment of inspection types to the order types,
materials to task list operations, objects to the
maintenance plan items and master inspection
characteristics to operations.

Q-66:   A. Incorrect class characteristic unit of
measure and B. Incorrect class characteristic assigned to
measuring point

A usage decision code for an inspection lot concludes
an inspection and documents its outcome. On the

basis of this code and its linkage to follow-up functions, the functions can be executed automatically. One such follow-up action is the creation of measurement documents to record inspection results for each inspection point that's defined for the test equipment. The critical values obtained by measurement readings are recorded in the documents and used to monitor a technical installation. The measurement documents are stored in the test equipment master record. The requirements for this functionality include the linkage of master inspection characteristics in the maintenance task list to measuring point master records by means of the class characteristics, as well as the creation of measuring point categories. Also required is the assignment of qualitative characteristics to the measuring point.

Q-67:   B. Measuring point assigned to equipment

A usage decision code for an inspection lot concludes an inspection and documents its outcome. On the basis of this code and its linkage to follow-up functions, the functions can be executed automatically. One such follow-up action is the creation of measurement documents to record inspection results for each inspection point that's defined for the test equipment. The critical values obtained by measurement readings are recorded in the documents and used to monitor a technical installation. The measurement documents are stored in the test equipment master record. The requirements for this functionality include the linkage of master inspection characteristics in the maintenance task list to measuring point master records by means of the class characteristics, as well as the creation of measuring point categories. Also required is the assignment of qualitative characteristics to the measuring point.

Q-68:   A. Plant Maintenance - Preventive Maintenance, C. Plant Maintenance - Maintenance Processing and D. Quality Management - Quality Inspections

The planning, scheduling and processing of calibration inspections require the functions of the Test Equipment Management component, as well as those of the Technical Objects, Preventive Maintenance and Maintenance Processing Plant Maintenance components. Also required are functions of the Quality Planning and Quality Inspection Quality Management components, in addition to the functions of the Classification System.

Q-69:   B. Schedule maintenance plan and D. Create maintenance plan for maintenance strategy

Test equipment is regularly inspected and calibrated to ensure it adheres to predefined performance criteria and is suitable for quality inspections. The results of the calibration inspection govern the release of the test equipment for subsequent use. The planning, scheduling and performance of calibration inspections require the master data, as well as the planning and processing functions of the Quality Management and Plant Maintenance components. For example, the inspection planning functions required to process a calibration inspection include creating equipment master records and test equipment groups, linking master inspection characteristics to class characteristics using the classification system and defining inspection specifications for both quantitative and qualitative characteristics. Additional planning functions include creating inspection characteristics for the maintenance task list operations and maintenance cycles in the maintenance plan, monitoring maintenance schedules and the status of the test equipment, and creating and releasing maintenance orders. In turn, the inspection processing functions include documenting inspection results for each piece of test equipment and creating maintenance notifications. valuating test equipment in an inspection lot, entering the usage decision for the inspection lot and confirming services for maintenance orders. Additional processing functions include conducting follow-up actions for an inspection lot usage decision and updating the Plant Maintenance and Quality Management Information Systems.

Q-70:   A. Maintenance plan may be defined with or without a maintenance strategy and B. Maintenance plan may be time- and/or performance-based

A maintenance plan is the central planning object for a calibration inspection. Maintenance plan items control the maintenance and inspection tasks that are performed on maintenance objects. These items control when maintenance or inspection tasks are performed using maintenance cycles for which time and performance-based inspection intervals are defined. Depending on Customizing settings, as a maintenance

plan is scheduled, maintenance calls are created and converted to orders when the calls are due. As the order that defines activities to be performed at a work station is released, an inspection lot is created and the maintenance task list, which determines the maintenance activities to be performed, is selected and assigned to the maintenance plan. Each task list structure contains operations and possibly sub-operations that describe the work to be performed during a calibration inspection. Inspection characteristics that describe what will be inspected using quantitative or qualitative inspection specifications can be assigned to the task list. Following the selection and assignment of the task list, the calibration inspection operations are performed in chronological order and characteristic inspection results are recorded and valuated. Next, based on the valuation of the inspection characteristics, a usage decision for the inspection lot is documented and the inspection lot is completed. The completion of the calibration inspection triggers an update to the test equipment status in the equipment master record to reflect the test equipment valuation as indicated by the lot's usage decision. In turn, the activities of the calibration inspection are confirmed for the maintenance order.

Q-71:   B. Maintenance plan

A maintenance plan is the central planning object for a calibration inspection. Maintenance plan items control the maintenance and inspection tasks that are performed on maintenance objects. These items control when maintenance or inspection tasks are

performed using maintenance cycles for which time and performance-based inspection intervals are defined. Depending on Customizing settings, as a maintenance plan is scheduled, maintenance calls are created and converted to orders when the calls are due. As an order is released, an inspection lot is created and the maintenance task list is selected and assigned to the maintenance plan. Each task list structure contains operations and possibly sub-operations that describe the work to be performed during a calibration inspection. Inspection characteristics that describe what will be inspected using quantitative or qualitative inspection specifications can be assigned to the task list. Following the selection and assignment of the task list, the calibration inspection operations are performed in chronological order and characteristic inspection results are recorded and valuated. Next, based on the valuation of the inspection characteristics, a usage decision for the inspection lot is documented and the inspection lot is completed. The completion of the calibration inspection triggers an update to the test equipment status in the equipment master record to reflect the test equipment valuation as indicated by the lot's usage decision. In turn, the activities of the calibration inspection are confirmed for the maintenance order.

Q-72:   B. Equipment master record, C. Task list and D. Maintenance plan

Test equipment is regularly inspected and calibrated to ensure that it adheres to predefined performance criteria is suitable for quality inspections. The results of

the calibration inspection govern the release of the test equipment for subsequent use. The planning, scheduling and performance of calibration inspections require the master data, as well as the planning and processing functions of the Test Equipment Management component. In particular, the functions required to plan a calibration inspection include the creation of an equipment master record, measuring points with reference to class characteristics and a maintenance strategy. Also required are the creation of a task list, an inspection lot, master inspection characteristics and a maintenance plan. In turn, Customizing requirements include the definition of an inspection type, inspection points, default values for the inspection type and an order type. Also required are the assignment of inspection types to the order types, materials to task list operations, objects to the maintenance plan items and master inspection characteristics to operations.

Q-73: A. The maintenance strategy enables a time-based or performance-based maintenance plan to be executed on a recurring basis

A maintenance plan is the central planning object for a calibration inspection. For example, a maintenance plan with a maintenance strategy enables time or performance-based maintenance plan to be executed on a recurring basis. Maintenance plan items control the maintenance and inspection tasks that are performed on maintenance objects. These items control when maintenance or inspection tasks are performed using maintenance cycles for which time and performance-based inspection intervals are defined. Depending on

174

Customizing settings, as a maintenance plan is scheduled, maintenance calls are created and converted to orders when the calls are due. As an order is released, an inspection lot is created and the maintenance task list is selected and assigned to the maintenance plan. Each task list structure contains operations and possibly sub-operations that describe the work to be performed during a calibration inspection. Inspection characteristics that describe what will be inspected using quantitative or qualitative inspection specifications can be assigned to the task list. Following the selection and assignment of the task list, the calibration inspection operations are performed in chronological order and characteristic inspection results are recorded and valuated. Next, based on the valuation of the inspection characteristics, a usage decision for the inspection lot is documented and the inspection lot is completed. The completion of the calibration inspection triggers an update to the test equipment status in the equipment master record to reflect the test equipment valuation as indicated by the lot's usage decision. In turn, the activities of the calibration inspection are confirmed for the maintenance order.

Q-74:   A. Maintenance cycle defined for a maintenance plan

A maintenance plan is the central planning object for a calibration inspection. Maintenance plan items control the maintenance and inspection tasks that are performed on maintenance objects. These items control when maintenance or inspection tasks are performed using maintenance cycles for which time and performance-based inspection intervals are defined. Depending on Customizing settings, as a maintenance plan is scheduled, maintenance calls are created and converted to orders when the calls are due. As an order is released, an inspection lot is created and the maintenance task list is selected and assigned to the maintenance plan. Each task list structure contains operations and possibly sub-operations that describe the work to be performed during a calibration inspection. Inspection characteristics that describe what will be inspected using quantitative or qualitative inspection specifications can be assigned to the task list. Following the selection and assignment of the task list, the calibration inspection operations are performed in chronological order and characteristic inspection results are recorded and valuated. Next, based on the valuation of the inspection characteristics, a usage decision for the inspection lot is documented and the inspection lot is completed. The completion of the calibration inspection triggers an update to the test equipment status in the equipment master record to reflect the test equipment valuation as indicated by the lot's usage decision. In turn, the activities of the calibration inspection are confirmed for the maintenance order.

Q-75:   C. Schedule maintenance plan

A maintenance plan is the central planning object for a calibration inspection. Maintenance plan items control the maintenance and inspection tasks that are performed on maintenance objects. These items control when maintenance or inspection tasks are

performed using maintenance cycles for which time and performance-based inspection intervals are defined. Depending on Customizing settings, as a maintenance plan is scheduled, maintenance calls are created and converted to orders when the calls are due. As an order is released, an inspection lot is created and the maintenance task list is selected and assigned to the maintenance plan. Each task list structure contains operations and possibly sub-operations that describe the work to be performed during a calibration inspection. Inspection characteristics that describe what will be inspected using quantitative or qualitative inspection specifications can be assigned to the task list. Following the selection and assignment of the task list, the calibration inspection operations are performed in chronological order and characteristic inspection results are recorded and valuated. Next, based on the valuation of the inspection characteristics, a usage decision for the inspection lot is documented and the inspection lot is completed. The completion of the calibration inspection triggers an update to the test equipment status in the equipment master record to reflect the test equipment valuation as indicated by the lot's usage decision. In turn, the activities of the calibration inspection are confirmed for the maintenance order.

Q-76:   A. Create task list and C. Create measuring points, counters and measurement documents

Test equipment is regularly inspected and calibrated to ensure that it adheres to predefined performance criteria is suitable for quality inspections. The results of

the calibration inspection govern the release of the test equipment for subsequent use. The planning, scheduling and performance of calibration inspections require the master data, as well as the planning and processing functions of the Test Equipment Management component. In particular, the functions required to plan a calibration inspection include the creation of an equipment master record, measuring points with reference to class characteristics and a maintenance strategy. Also required are the creation of a task list, an inspection lot, master inspection characteristics and a maintenance plan. In turn, Customizing requirements include the definition of an inspection type, inspection points, default values for the inspection type and an order type. Also required are the assignment of inspection types to the order types, materials to task list operations, objects to the maintenance plan items and master inspection characteristics to operations.

Q-77:   A. Record Results

Test equipment is regularly inspected and calibrated to ensure that the equipment adheres to predefined performance criteria. The planning, scheduling and performance of calibration inspections require the master data, as well as the planning and processing functions of the Test Equipment Management component. The calibration inspection processing functions include inspecting the test equipment, processing the maintenance order, recording calibration inspection results and creating and processing notifications. Other processing functions are entering the usage decision for the calibration inspection, executing follow-up actions and completing the maintenance order.

Q-78:   C. Sampling procedure

The quality of the items in an inspection lot can be evaluated on the basis of an inspection of samples, each of which can be selected by means of a sampling procedure. The two primary elements of a sampling procedure are the sampling type and the valuation mode. The sampling type controls the calculation of the sample size. In turn, the valuation mode specifies the rules that are used to determine if, following an inspection, a characteristic or sample is accepted or rejected for its intended purpose. The valuation rules are defined on the basis of the characteristic category and the sampling procedure that's assigned to the inspection characteristic. Examples of a valuation mode include the attributive inspection according to the number of nonconforming units, the variable inspection with a single-sided or double-sided tolerance range and the inspection without valuations parameters. If a characteristic is valuated on the wrong basis, the Change Valuation Mode function is used to select a different valuation mode.

Q-79:   A. Valuation mode

The quality of the items in an inspection lot can be evaluated on the basis of an inspection of samples, each of which can be selected by means of a sampling procedure. The two primary elements of a sampling procedure are the sampling type and the valuation mode. The sampling type controls the calculation of the sample size. In turn, the valuation mode specifies the rules that are used to determine if, following an inspection, a characteristic or sample is accepted or rejected for its intended purpose. The valuation rules are defined on the basis of the characteristic category and the sampling procedure that's assigned to the inspection characteristic. Examples of a valuation mode include the attributive inspection according to the number of nonconforming units, the variable inspection with a single-sided or double-sided tolerance range and the inspection without valuations parameters. If a characteristic is valuated on the wrong basis, the Change Valuation Mode function is used to select a different valuation mode.

Q-80:   A. Performance

A maintenance plan is the central planning object for a calibration inspection. Maintenance plan items control the maintenance and inspection tasks that are performed on maintenance objects. These items control when maintenance or inspection tasks are performed using maintenance cycles for which time and performance-based inspection intervals are defined. Depending on Customizing settings, as a maintenance plan is scheduled, maintenance calls are created and converted to orders when the calls are due. As an order is released, an inspection lot is created and the maintenance task list is selected and assigned to the maintenance plan. Each task list structure contains operations and possibly sub-operations that describe the work to be performed during a calibration inspection. Inspection characteristics that describe what will be inspected using quantitative or qualitative inspection specifications can be assigned to the task list. Following the selection and assignment of the task list, the calibration inspection operations are performed in chronological order and characteristic inspection results are recorded and valuated. Next, based on the valuation of the inspection characteristics, a usage decision for the inspection lot is documented and the inspection lot is completed. The completion of the calibration inspection triggers an update to the test equipment status in the equipment master record to reflect the test equipment valuation as indicated by the lot's usage decision. In turn, the activities of the calibration inspection are confirmed for the maintenance order.

Q-81:   C. Maintenance plan

A maintenance plan is the central planning object for a calibration inspection. Maintenance plan items control the maintenance and inspection tasks that are performed on maintenance objects. These items control when maintenance or inspection tasks are performed using maintenance cycles for which time and performance-based inspection intervals are defined. Depending on Customizing settings, as a maintenance plan is scheduled, maintenance calls are created and converted to orders when the calls are due. As an order is released, an inspection lot is created and the maintenance task list is selected and assigned to the maintenance plan. Each task list structure contains operations and possibly sub-operations that describe the work to be performed during a calibration inspection. Inspection characteristics that describe what will be inspected using quantitative or qualitative inspection specifications can be assigned to the task list. Following the selection and assignment of the task list, the calibration inspection operations are performed in chronological order and characteristic inspection results are recorded and valuated. Next, based on the valuation of the inspection characteristics, a usage decision for the inspection lot is documented and the inspection lot is completed. The completion of the calibration inspection triggers an update to the test equipment status in the equipment master record to reflect the test equipment valuation as indicated by the lot's usage decision. In turn, the activities of the calibration inspection are confirmed for the maintenance order.

Q-82: B. Define the individual steps of a calibration inspection in greater detail than would be possible if an operation were used

A maintenance plan is the central planning object for a calibration inspection. Maintenance plan items control the maintenance and inspection tasks that are performed on maintenance objects. These items control when maintenance or inspection tasks are performed using maintenance cycles for which time and performance-based inspection intervals are defined. Depending on Customizing settings, as a maintenance plan is scheduled, maintenance calls are created and converted to orders when the calls are due. As an order is released, an inspection lot is created and the maintenance task list is selected and assigned to the maintenance plan. Each task list structure contains operations and possibly sub-operations that describe the work to be performed during a calibration inspection. Inspection characteristics that describe what will be inspected using quantitative or qualitative inspection specifications can be assigned to the task list. Following the selection and assignment of the task list, the calibration inspection operations are performed in chronological order and characteristic inspection results are recorded and valuated. Next, based on the valuation of the inspection characteristics, a usage decision for the inspection lot is documented and the inspection lot is completed. The completion of the calibration inspection triggers an update to the test equipment status in the equipment master record to reflect the test equipment valuation as indicated by the lot's usage decision. In turn, the activities of the calibration inspection are confirmed for the maintenance order.

Q-83:   C. Maintenance order

A maintenance plan is the central planning object for a calibration inspection. Maintenance plan items control the maintenance and inspection tasks that are performed on maintenance objects. These items control when maintenance or inspection tasks are performed using maintenance cycles for which time and performance-based inspection intervals are defined. Depending on Customizing settings, as a maintenance plan is scheduled, maintenance calls are created and converted to orders when the calls are due. As an order is released, an inspection lot is created and the maintenance task list – equipment, functional or general task list -- is selected and assigned to the maintenance plan. Each task list structure contains operations and possibly sub-operations that describe the work to be performed during a calibration inspection. Inspection characteristics that describe what will be inspected using quantitative or qualitative inspection specifications can be assigned to the task list. Following the selection and assignment of the task list, the calibration inspection operations are performed in chronological order and characteristic inspection results are recorded and valuated. Next, based on the valuation of the inspection characteristics, a usage decision for the inspection lot is documented and the inspection lot is completed. The completion of the calibration inspection triggers an update to the test equipment status in the equipment master record to reflect the test equipment valuation as indicated by the lot's usage decision. In turn, the activities of the calibration inspection are confirmed for the maintenance order.

Q-84:   B. Inspection lot is to be created automatically as a maintenance order is released

Test equipment is regularly inspected and calibrated to ensure that it adheres to predefined performance criteria is suitable for quality inspections. The results of the calibration inspection govern the release of the test equipment for subsequent use. The planning, scheduling and performance of calibration inspections require the master data, as well as the planning and processing functions of the Test Equipment Management component. In particular, the functions required to plan a calibration inspection include the creation of an equipment master record, measuring points with reference to class characteristics and a maintenance strategy. Also required are the creation of a task list, an inspection lot, master inspection characteristics and a maintenance plan. In turn, Customizing requirements include the definition of an inspection type, inspection points, default values for the inspection type and an order type. Also required are the assignment of inspection types to the order types, materials to task list operations, objects to the maintenance plan items and master inspection characteristics to operations.

Q-85:   B. Class characteristic is not assigned to measuring point/counter and master inspection characteristic

A usage decision code for an inspection lot concludes an inspection and documents its outcome. On the basis of this code and its linkage to follow-up functions, the functions can be executed automatically. One such follow-up action is the creation of measurement documents to record inspection results for each inspection point that's defined for the test equipment. The critical values obtained by measurement readings are recorded in the documents and used to monitor a technical installation. The measurement documents are stored in the test equipment master record. The requirements for this functionality include the linkage of master inspection characteristics in the maintenance task list to measuring point master records by means of the class characteristics, as well as the creation of measuring point categories. Also required is the assignment of qualitative characteristics to the measuring point.

Q-86:   B. Maintenance task list

A maintenance plan is the central planning object for a calibration inspection. Maintenance plan items control the maintenance and inspection tasks that are performed on maintenance objects. These items control when maintenance or inspection tasks are performed using maintenance cycles for which time and performance-based inspection intervals are defined. Depending on Customizing settings, as a maintenance plan is scheduled, maintenance calls are created and converted to orders when the calls are due. As an order is released, an inspection lot is created and the maintenance task list is selected and assigned to the maintenance plan. Each task list structure contains operations and possibly sub-operations that describe the tasks to be performed during a calibration inspection. Inspection characteristics that describe what will be inspected using quantitative or qualitative inspection specifications can be assigned to the task list. Following the selection and assignment of the task list, the calibration inspection operations are performed in chronological order and characteristic inspection results are recorded and valuated. Next, based on the valuation of the inspection characteristics, a usage decision for the inspection lot is documented and the inspection lot is completed. The completion of the calibration inspection triggers an update to the test equipment status in the equipment master record to reflect the test equipment valuation as indicated by the

lot's usage decision. In turn, the activities of the calibration inspection are confirmed for the maintenance order.

Q-87:   B. Maintenance task list

A maintenance plan is the central planning object for a calibration inspection. Maintenance plan items control the maintenance and inspection tasks that are performed on maintenance objects. These items control when maintenance or inspection tasks are performed using maintenance cycles for which time and performance-based inspection intervals are defined. Depending on Customizing settings, as a maintenance plan is scheduled, maintenance calls are created and converted to orders when the calls are due. As an order is released, an inspection lot is created and the maintenance task list is selected and assigned to the maintenance plan. Each task list structure contains operations and possibly sub-operations that describe the work to be performed during a calibration inspection. Inspection characteristics that describe what will be inspected using quantitative or qualitative inspection specifications can be assigned to the task list. Following the selection and assignment of the task list, the calibration inspection operations are performed in chronological order and characteristic inspection results are recorded and valuated. Next, based on the valuation of the inspection characteristics, a usage decision for the inspection lot is documented and the inspection lot is completed. The completion of the calibration inspection triggers an update to the test equipment status in the equipment master record to

reflect the test equipment valuation as indicated by the lot's usage decision. In turn, the activities of the calibration inspection are confirmed for the maintenance order.

Q-88:   A. Plant Maintenance

The Plant Maintenance component is used to create an equipment master record for each piece of test equipment. This master record provides the means to manage test equipment at the client level, document the equipment's maintenance history, as well as the equipment's status, which the calibration inspection determines. The equipment master record is also used to maintain static information about the equipment, such as the equipment's acquisition value and dimensions and the date the equipment was acquired. Also in the master record are the equipment's manufacturer, the work center and plant at which the equipment is located, and the equipment's serial number and cost center. The equipment's maintenance intervals, which are either time or performance-based, are also stored in the equipment master record.

Q-89:   A. Update equipment status and E. Update measurement documents

A usage decision code for an inspection lot concludes an inspection and documents its outcome. On the basis of this code and its linkage to follow-up functions, the functions can be executed automatically. One such follow-up action is the creation of measurement documents to record inspection results for each inspection point that's defined for the test equipment. The critical values obtained by measurement readings are recorded in the documents and used to monitor a technical installation. The measurement documents are stored in the test equipment master record. The requirements for this functionality include the linkage of master inspection characteristics in the maintenance task list to measuring point master records by means of the class characteristics, as well as the creation of measuring point categories. Also required is the assignment of qualitative characteristics to the measuring point.

Q-90:   B. Time-based maintenance plan with maintenance strategy and C. Single-cycle time-based maintenance plan

A maintenance plan is the central planning object for a calibration inspection. Maintenance plan items control the maintenance and inspection tasks that are performed on maintenance objects. These items control when maintenance or inspection tasks are performed using maintenance cycles for which time and performance-based inspection intervals are defined. Both a time-based maintenance plan with maintenance strategy and single-cycle time-based maintenance plan are used to schedule maintenance tasks on a time basis. Depending on Customizing settings, as a maintenance plan is scheduled, maintenance calls are created and converted to orders when the calls are due. As an order is released, an inspection lot is created and the maintenance task list is selected and assigned to the maintenance plan. Each task list structure contains

operations and possibly sub-operations that describe the work to be performed during a calibration inspection. Inspection characteristics that describe what will be inspected using quantitative or qualitative inspection specifications can be assigned to the task list. Following the selection and assignment of the task list, the calibration inspection operations are performed in chronological order and characteristic inspection results are recorded and valuated. Next, based on the valuation of the inspection characteristics, a usage decision for the inspection lot is documented and the inspection lot is completed. The completion of the calibration inspection triggers an update to the test equipment status in the equipment master record to reflect the test equipment valuation as indicated by the lot's usage decision. In turn, the activities of the calibration inspection are confirmed for the maintenance order.

Q-91:   A. Materials assigned to maintenance task list operation and C. Master inspection characteristic assigned to operation

Test equipment is regularly inspected and calibrated to ensure that it adheres to predefined performance criteria is suitable for quality inspections. The results of the calibration inspection govern the release of the test equipment for subsequent use. The planning, scheduling and performance of calibration inspections require the master data, as well as the planning and processing functions of the Test Equipment Management component. In particular, the functions required to plan a calibration inspection include the creation of an equipment master record, measuring points with reference to class characteristics and a maintenance strategy. Also required are the creation of a task list, an inspection lot, master inspection characteristics and a maintenance plan. In turn, Customizing requirements include the definition of an inspection type, inspection points, default values for the inspection type and an order type. Also required are the assignment of inspection types to the order types, materials to task list operations, objects to the maintenance plan items and master inspection characteristics to operations.

Q-92:   C. Inspection characteristic

The quality of the items in an inspection lot can be evaluated on the basis of an inspection of samples, each of which can be selected by means of a sampling procedure. The two primary elements of a sampling procedure are the sampling type and the valuation mode. The sampling type controls the calculation of the sample size. In turn, the valuation mode specifies the rules that are used to determine if, following an inspection, a characteristic or sample is accepted or rejected for its intended purpose. The valuation rules are defined on the basis of the characteristic category and the sampling procedure that's assigned to the inspection characteristic. Examples of a valuation mode include the attributive inspection according to the number of nonconforming units, the variable inspection with a single-sided or double-sided tolerance range and the inspection without valuations parameters.

Q-93:   B. Assign qualitative characteristic with a
selected set to the measuring point

A usage decision code for an inspection lot concludes
an inspection and documents its outcome. On the
basis of this code and its linkage to follow-up functions,
the functions can be executed automatically. One such
follow-up action is the creation of measurement
documents to record inspection results for each
inspection point that's defined for the test equipment.
The critical values obtained by measurement readings
are recorded in the documents and used to monitor a
technical installation. The measurement documents are
stored in the test equipment master record. The
requirements for this functionality include the linkage
of master inspection characteristics in the maintenance
task list to measuring point master records by means of
the class characteristics, as well as the creation of
measuring point categories. Also required is the
assignment of qualitative characteristics to the
measuring point.

Q-94:   A. Equipment master record

The Plant Maintenance component is used to create an
equipment master record for each piece of test
equipment. This master record provides the means to
manage test equipment at the client level, document the
equipment's maintenance history, as well as the
equipment's status, which the calibration inspection
determines. The equipment master record is also used
to maintain static information about the equipment,
such as the equipment's acquisition value and
dimensions and the date the equipment was acquired.

Also in the master record are the equipment's manufacturer, the work center and plant at which the equipment is located, and the equipment's serial number and cost center. The equipment's maintenance intervals, which are either time or performance-based, are also stored in the equipment master record.

Q-95:   A. Test equipment

The Plant Maintenance component is used to create an equipment master record for each piece of test equipment. This master record provides the means to manage test equipment at the client level, document the equipment's maintenance history, as well as the equipment's status, which the calibration inspection determines. The equipment master record is also used to maintain static information about the equipment, such as the equipment's acquisition value and dimensions and the date the equipment was acquired. Also in the master record are the equipment's manufacturer, the work center and plant at which the equipment is located, and the equipment's serial number and cost center. The equipment's maintenance intervals, which are either time or performance-based, are also stored in the equipment master record.

Q-96:   B. Time-based maintenance plan with maintenance strategy

A maintenance plan is the central planning object for a calibration inspection. The time-based maintenance plan with maintenance strategy is used to plan recurring calibration inspections on a time basis. Maintenance plan items control the maintenance and inspection tasks that are performed on maintenance objects. These items control when maintenance or inspection tasks are performed using maintenance cycles for which time and performance-based inspection intervals are defined. Depending on Customizing settings, as a maintenance plan is scheduled, maintenance calls are created and converted to orders when the calls are due. As an order is released, an inspection lot is created and the maintenance task list is selected and assigned to the maintenance plan. Each task list structure contains operations and possibly sub-operations that describe the work to be performed during a calibration inspection. Inspection characteristics that describe what will be inspected using quantitative or qualitative inspection specifications can be assigned to the task list. Following the selection and assignment of the task list, the calibration inspection operations are performed in chronological order and characteristic inspection results are recorded and valuated. Next, based on the valuation of the inspection characteristics, a usage decision for the inspection lot is documented and the inspection lot is completed. The completion of the calibration inspection triggers an update to the test equipment status in the equipment master record to reflect the test equipment valuation as indicated by the lot's usage decision. In turn, the activities of the calibration inspection are confirmed for the maintenance order.

Q-97:   A. Maintenance order

A maintenance plan is the central planning object for a calibration inspection. Maintenance plan items control the maintenance and inspection tasks that are performed on maintenance objects. These items control when maintenance or inspection tasks are performed using maintenance cycles for which time and performance-based inspection intervals are defined. Depending on Customizing settings, as a maintenance plan is scheduled, maintenance calls are created and converted to orders when the calls are due. The order documents required maintenance tasks as well as define the work center at which the tasks will be performed As an order is released, an inspection lot is created and the maintenance task list is selected and assigned to the maintenance plan. Each task list structure contains operations and possibly sub-operations that describe the work to be performed during a calibration inspection. Inspection characteristics that describe what will be inspected using quantitative or qualitative inspection specifications can be assigned to the task list. Following the selection and assignment of the task list, the calibration inspection operations are performed in chronological order and characteristic inspection results are recorded and valuated. Next, based on the valuation of the inspection characteristics, a usage decision for the inspection lot is documented and the inspection lot is completed. The completion of the calibration inspection triggers an update to the test equipment status in the equipment master record to reflect the test equipment valuation as indicated by the lot's usage decision. In turn, the activities of the calibration inspection are confirmed for the

maintenance order using either the Results Recording or Inspection Lot Completion functions.

Q-98:   E. Any of the above

The Controlling component uses orders to plan, monitor and settle operating costs. The maintenance order is the means by which activities that support calibration inspections are linked to cost assignment objects in the Controlling component. Like all costs accounted for by the Controlling component, test equipment maintenance costs are classified according to the functional origin of the cost by means of an order category. The functional origin of the costs is indicated by the order category 30. In turn, the 14 order type is used to collect costs that originate with calibration inspection activities. Each inspection activity is recorded in terms of an activity type and activity times. The CO component then identifies the predefined price associated with the activity type. The CO component converts the activity time to an actual cost on the basis of the predefined price stored in the CO component. The calibration inspection costs are then settled to a cost object according to the account assignment that's entered when the order was created. During settlement, the actual costs incurred to conduct the inspection are allocated to one or more receivers. The system then automatically generates offsetting entries to the sender objects and the debit postings to the sender object remain in place.

Q-99:   A. Operations are performed in chronological order

A maintenance plan is the central planning object for a calibration inspection. Maintenance plan items control the maintenance and inspection tasks that are performed on maintenance objects. These items control when maintenance or inspection tasks are performed using maintenance cycles for which time and performance-based inspection intervals are defined. Depending on Customizing settings, as a maintenance plan is scheduled, maintenance calls are created and converted to orders when the calls are due. As an order is released, an inspection lot is created and the maintenance task list is selected and assigned to the maintenance plan. Each task list structure contains operations and possibly sub-operations that describe the work to be performed during a calibration inspection. Inspection characteristics that describe what will be inspected using quantitative or qualitative inspection specifications can be assigned to the task list. Following the selection and assignment of the task list, the calibration inspection operations are performed in chronological order and characteristic inspection results are recorded and valuated. Next, based on the valuation of the inspection characteristics, a usage decision for the inspection lot is documented and the inspection lot is completed. The completion of the calibration inspection triggers an update to the test equipment status in the equipment master record to reflect the test equipment valuation as indicated by the lot's usage decision. In turn, the activities of the calibration inspection are confirmed for the maintenance order.

Q-100:   A. Operation in maintenance task list

A maintenance plan is the central planning object for a calibration inspection. Maintenance plan items control the maintenance and inspection tasks that are performed on maintenance objects. These items control when maintenance or inspection tasks are performed using maintenance cycles for which time and performance-based inspection intervals are defined. Depending on Customizing settings, as a maintenance plan is scheduled, maintenance calls are created and converted to orders when the calls are due. As an order is released, an inspection lot is created and the maintenance task list is selected and assigned to the maintenance plan. Each task list structure contains operations and possibly sub-operations that describe the work to be performed during a calibration inspection. Inspection characteristics that describe what will be inspected using quantitative or qualitative inspection specifications can be assigned to operations in the task list. Following the selection and assignment of the task list, the calibration inspection operations are performed in chronological order and characteristic inspection results are recorded and valuated. Next, based on the valuation of the inspection characteristics, a usage decision for the inspection lot is documented and the inspection lot is completed. The completion of the calibration inspection triggers an update to the test equipment status in the equipment master record to reflect the test equipment valuation as indicated by the lot's usage decision. In turn, the activities of the calibration inspection are confirmed for the maintenance order.

Q-101:   A. Planning

Test equipment is regularly inspected and calibrated to ensure that it adheres to predefined performance criteria is suitable for quality inspections. The results of the calibration inspection govern the release of the test equipment for subsequent use. The planning, scheduling and performance of calibration inspections require the master data, as well as the planning and processing functions of the Test Equipment Management component. In particular, the functions required to plan a calibration inspection include the creation of an equipment master record, measuring points with reference to class characteristics and a maintenance strategy. Also required are the creation of a task list, an inspection lot, master inspection characteristics and a maintenance plan. In turn, Customizing requirements include the definition of an inspection type, inspection points, default values for the inspection type and an order type. Also required are the assignment of inspection types to the order types, materials to task list operations, objects to the maintenance plan items and master inspection characteristics to operations.

Q-102:   D. Determines the quality costs settlement rules

The Controlling component uses orders to plan, monitor and settle operating costs. The maintenance order is the means by which activities that support calibration inspections are linked to cost assignment objects in the Controlling component. Like all costs accounted for by the Controlling component, test equipment maintenance costs are classified according to the functional origin of the cost by means of an order category. The functional origin of the costs is indicated by the order category 30. In turn, the 14 order type is used to collect costs that originate with calibration inspection activities. Each inspection activity is recorded in terms of an activity type and activity times. The CO component then identifies the predefined price associated with the activity type. The CO component converts the activity time to an actual cost on the basis of the predefined price stored in the CO component. The calibration inspection costs are then settled to a cost object according to the account assignment that's entered when the order was created. During settlement, the actual costs incurred to conduct the inspection are allocated to one or more receivers. The system then automatically generates offsetting entries to the sender objects and the debit postings to the sender object remain in place.

Q-103:   B. Maintenance plan

A maintenance plan is the central planning object for a calibration inspection. Maintenance plan items control the maintenance and inspection tasks that are performed on maintenance objects. These items control when maintenance or inspection tasks are performed using maintenance cycles for which time and performance-based inspection intervals are defined. Depending on Customizing settings, as a maintenance plan is scheduled, maintenance calls are created and converted to orders when the calls are due. As an order is released, an inspection lot is created and the maintenance task list is selected and assigned to the

maintenance plan. Each task list structure contains operations and possibly sub-operations that describe the work to be performed during a calibration inspection. Inspection characteristics that describe what will be inspected using quantitative or qualitative inspection specifications can be assigned to the task list. Following the selection and assignment of the task list, the calibration inspection operations are performed in chronological order and characteristic inspection results are recorded and valuated. Next, based on the valuation of the inspection characteristics, a usage decision for the inspection lot is documented and the inspection lot is completed. The completion of the calibration inspection triggers an update to the test equipment status in the equipment master record to reflect the test equipment valuation as indicated by the lot's usage decision. In turn, the activities of the calibration inspection are confirmed for the maintenance order.

Q-104:   A. Operation and B. Sub-operation

A maintenance plan is the central planning object for a calibration inspection. Maintenance plan items control the maintenance and inspection tasks that are performed on maintenance objects. These items control when maintenance or inspection tasks are performed using maintenance cycles for which time and performance-based inspection intervals are defined. Depending on Customizing settings, as a maintenance plan is scheduled, maintenance calls are created and converted to orders when the calls are due. As an order is released, an inspection lot is created and the maintenance task list is selected and assigned to the

maintenance plan. Each task list structure contains operations and possibly sub-operations that describe the work to be performed during a calibration inspection. Inspection characteristics that describe what will be inspected using quantitative or qualitative inspection specifications can be assigned to the task list. Following the selection and assignment of the task list, the calibration inspection operations are performed in chronological order and characteristic inspection results are recorded and valuated. Next, based on the valuation of the inspection characteristics, a usage decision for the inspection lot is documented and the inspection lot is completed. The completion of the calibration inspection triggers an update to the test equipment status in the equipment master record to reflect the test equipment valuation as indicated by the lot's usage decision. In turn, the activities of the calibration inspection are confirmed for the maintenance order.

Q-105:   A. Maintenance order

A maintenance plan is the central planning object for a calibration inspection. Maintenance plan items control the maintenance and inspection tasks that are performed on maintenance objects by internal or external stakeholders. These items control when maintenance or inspection tasks are performed using maintenance cycles for which time and performance-based inspection intervals are defined. Depending on Customizing settings, as a maintenance plan is scheduled, maintenance calls are created and converted to orders when the calls are due. As an order is released, an inspection lot is created and the maintenance task list is selected and assigned to the maintenance plan. Each task list structure contains operations and possibly sub-operations that describe the work to be performed during a calibration inspection. Inspection characteristics that describe what will be inspected using quantitative or qualitative inspection specifications can be assigned to the task list. Following the selection and assignment of the task list, the calibration inspection operations are performed in chronological order and characteristic inspection results are recorded and valuated. Next, based on the valuation of the inspection characteristics, a usage decision for the inspection lot is documented and the inspection lot is completed. The completion of the calibration inspection triggers an update to the test equipment status in the equipment master record to reflect the test equipment valuation as indicated by the lot's usage decision. In turn, the activities of the calibration inspection are confirmed for the maintenance order using either the Results Recording or Inspection Lot Completion functions.

Q-106:   A. Equipment master record created

Test equipment is regularly inspected and calibrated to ensure that it adheres to predefined performance criteria is suitable for quality inspections. The results of the calibration inspection govern the release of the test equipment for subsequent use. The planning, scheduling and performance of calibration inspections require the master data, as well as the planning and processing functions of the Test Equipment

Management component. In particular, the functions required to plan a calibration inspection include the creation of an equipment master record, measuring points with reference to class characteristics and a maintenance strategy. Also required are the creation of a task list, an inspection lot, master inspection characteristics and a maintenance plan. In turn, Customizing requirements include the definition of an inspection type, inspection points, default values for the inspection type and an order type. Also required are the assignment of inspection types to the order types, materials to task list operations, objects to the maintenance plan items and master inspection characteristics to operations.

Q-107:   C. Processing

The planning, scheduling and performance of calibration inspections require the master data and the planning and processing functions of the Test Equipment Management component. These functions include the inspection of test equipment, processing the maintenance order and recording the calibration inspection results. Also required are creating and processing notifications, entering the usage decision for the calibration inspection, executing follow-up actions and completing the maintenance order.

Q-108:   B. Create master inspection characteristic and C. Create equipment master record

Test equipment is regularly inspected and calibrated to ensure that it adheres to predefined performance criteria is suitable for quality inspections. The results of the calibration inspection govern the release of the test equipment for subsequent use. The planning, scheduling and performance of calibration inspections require the master data, as well as the planning and processing functions of the Test Equipment Management component. In particular, the functions required to plan a calibration inspection include the creation of an equipment master record, measuring points with reference to class characteristics and a maintenance strategy. Also required are the creation of a task list, an inspection lot, master inspection characteristics and a maintenance plan. In turn, Customizing requirements include the definition of an inspection type, inspection points, default values for the inspection type and an order type. Also required are the assignment of inspection types to the order types, materials to task list operations, objects to the maintenance plan items and master inspection characteristics to operations.

Q-109: A. Maintenance plan item

A maintenance plan is the central planning object for a calibration inspection. Maintenance plan items control the maintenance and inspection tasks that are performed on maintenance objects. These items control when maintenance or inspection tasks are performed using maintenance cycles for which time and performance-based inspection intervals are defined. Depending on Customizing settings, as a maintenance plan is scheduled, maintenance calls are created and converted to orders when the calls are due. As an order is released, an inspection lot is created and the maintenance task list is selected and assigned to the maintenance plan. Each task list structure contains operations and possibly sub-operations that describe the work to be performed during a calibration inspection. Inspection characteristics that describe what will be inspected using quantitative or qualitative inspection specifications can be assigned to the task list. Following the selection and assignment of the task list, the calibration inspection operations are performed in chronological order and characteristic inspection results are recorded and valuated. Next, based on the valuation of the inspection characteristics, a usage decision for the inspection lot is documented and the inspection lot is completed. The completion of the calibration inspection triggers an update to the test equipment status in the equipment master record to reflect the test equipment valuation as indicated by the lot's usage decision. In turn, the activities of the calibration inspection are confirmed for the maintenance order.

Q-110: A. Technical specifications

The Classification system is used to categorize test equipment according to the equipment's technical specifications. This system relies on the specifications to describe objects and then uses the descriptions to group the objects into classes. Doing so enables the search for objects on the basis of the descriptions or characteristics.

Q-111:   A. General maintenance task list

A maintenance plan is the central planning object for a calibration inspection. Maintenance plan items control the maintenance and inspection tasks that are performed on maintenance objects. These items control when maintenance or inspection tasks are performed using maintenance cycles for which time and performance-based inspection intervals are defined. Depending on Customizing settings, as a maintenance plan is scheduled, maintenance calls are created and converted to orders when the calls are due. As an order is released, an inspection lot is created and the maintenance task list – equipment, functional or general task list -- is selected and assigned to the maintenance plan. . The general maintenance task list in particular can be used to minimize the effort required to create a maintenance task list. Each task list structure contains operations and possibly sub-operations that describe the work to be performed during a calibration inspection. Inspection characteristics that describe what will be inspected using quantitative or qualitative inspection specifications can be assigned to the task list. Following the selection and assignment of the task list, the calibration inspection operations are performed in chronological order and characteristic inspection results are recorded and valuated. Next, based on the valuation of the inspection characteristics, a usage decision for the inspection lot is documented and the inspection lot is completed. The completion of the calibration inspection triggers an update to the test equipment status in the equipment master record to reflect the test equipment valuation as indicated by the

lot's usage decision. In turn, the activities of the calibration inspection are confirmed for the maintenance order.

Q-112: A. Assignment of a class characteristic with the required unit of measure to the measuring point

A usage decision code for an inspection lot concludes an inspection and documents its outcome. On the basis of this code and its linkage to follow-up functions, the functions can be executed automatically. One such follow-up action is the creation of measurement documents to record inspection results for each inspection point that's defined for the test equipment. The critical values obtained by measurement readings are recorded in the documents and used to monitor a technical installation. The measurement documents are stored in the test equipment master record. The requirements for this functionality include the linkage of master inspection characteristics in the maintenance task list to measuring point master records by means of the class characteristic with the required unit of measure, as well as the creation of measuring point categories.

Q-113: A. Maintenance order

A maintenance plan is the central planning object for a calibration inspection. Maintenance plan items control the maintenance and inspection tasks that are performed on maintenance objects. These items control when maintenance or inspection tasks are performed using maintenance cycles for which time and performance-based inspection intervals are defined.

Depending on Customizing settings, as a maintenance plan is scheduled, maintenance calls are created and converted to orders when the calls are due. As an order is released, an inspection lot is created and the maintenance task list is selected and assigned to the maintenance plan. Each task list structure contains operations and possibly sub-operations that describe the work to be performed during a calibration inspection. Inspection characteristics that describe what will be inspected using quantitative or qualitative inspection specifications can be assigned to the task list. Following the selection and assignment of the task list, the calibration inspection operations are performed in chronological order and characteristic inspection results are recorded and valuated. Next, based on the valuation of the inspection characteristics, a usage decision for the inspection lot is documented and the inspection lot is completed. The completion of the calibration inspection triggers an update to the test equipment status in the equipment master record to reflect the test equipment valuation as indicated by the lot's usage decision. In turn, the activities of the calibration inspection are confirmed for the maintenance order.

Q-114:   B. Maintenance plan includes maintenance calls that are released on due date

A maintenance plan is the central planning object for a calibration inspection. Maintenance plan items control the maintenance and inspection tasks that are performed on maintenance objects. These items control when maintenance or inspection tasks are

performed using maintenance cycles for which time and performance-based inspection intervals are defined. Depending on Customizing settings, as a maintenance plan is scheduled, maintenance calls are created and converted to orders when the calls are due. As an order is released, an inspection lot is created and the maintenance task list is selected and assigned to the maintenance plan. Each task list structure contains operations and possibly sub-operations that describe the work to be performed during a calibration inspection. Inspection characteristics that describe what will be inspected using quantitative or qualitative inspection specifications can be assigned to the task list. Following the selection and assignment of the task list, the calibration inspection operations are performed in chronological order and characteristic inspection results are recorded and valuated. Next, based on the valuation of the inspection characteristics, a usage decision for the inspection lot is documented and the inspection lot is completed. The completion of the calibration inspection triggers an update to the test equipment status in the equipment master record to reflect the test equipment valuation as indicated by the lot's usage decision. In turn, the activities of the calibration inspection are confirmed for the maintenance order. If an inspection is conducted without a maintenance plan, the order must be created using an order type that's linked to a QM inspection type.

Q-115:   D. Performance-based maintenance plan with maintenance strategy

A maintenance plan is the central planning object for a calibration inspection. Five types of maintenance plans are available. A maintenance plan with a maintenance strategy is time or performance-based. In turn, a maintenance plan without a maintenance strategy is a single-cycle time-based plan, a single-cycle performance-based plan or a multiple counter plan, which is time and performance-based. Maintenance plan items control the maintenance and inspection tasks that are performed on maintenance objects. These items control when maintenance or inspection tasks are performed using maintenance cycles for which time and performance-based inspection intervals are defined. Depending on Customizing settings, as a maintenance plan is scheduled, maintenance calls are created and converted to orders when the calls are due. As an order is released, an inspection lot is created and the maintenance task list is selected and assigned to the maintenance plan. Each task list structure contains operations and possibly sub-operations that describe the work to be performed during a calibration inspection. Inspection characteristics that describe what will be inspected using quantitative or qualitative inspection specifications can be assigned to the task list. Following the selection and assignment of the task list, the calibration inspection operations are performed in chronological order and characteristic inspection results are recorded and valuated. Next, based on the valuation of the inspection characteristics, a usage decision for the inspection lot is documented and the inspection lot is completed. The completion of the calibration inspection triggers an update to the test equipment status in the equipment master record to

reflect the test equipment valuation as indicated by the lot's usage decision. In turn, the activities of the calibration inspection are confirmed for the maintenance order.

Q-116: A. Maintenance task list

A maintenance plan is the central planning object for a calibration inspection. Maintenance plan items control the maintenance and inspection tasks that are performed on maintenance objects. These items control when maintenance or inspection tasks are performed using maintenance cycles for which time and performance-based inspection intervals are defined. Depending on Customizing settings, as a maintenance plan is scheduled, maintenance calls are created and converted to orders when the calls are due. As an order is released, an inspection lot, which determines the activities to be performed and the required resources, is created and the maintenance task list, which determines the maintenance activities to be performed and the materials and resources that are required to perform maintenance work, is selected and assigned to the maintenance plan. Each task list structure contains operations and possibly sub-operations that describe the work to be performed during a calibration inspection. Inspection characteristics that describe what will be inspected using quantitative or qualitative inspection specifications can be assigned to the task list. Following the selection and assignment of the task list, the calibration inspection operations are performed in chronological order and characteristic inspection results are recorded and valuated. Next, based on the valuation of the inspection characteristics, a usage

decision for the inspection lot is documented and the inspection lot is completed. The completion of the calibration inspection triggers an update to the test equipment status in the equipment master record to reflect the test equipment valuation as indicated by the lot's usage decision. In turn, the activities of the calibration inspection are confirmed for the maintenance order.

Q-117:   A. Definition of maintenance dates in the maintenance plan

A maintenance plan is the central planning object for a calibration inspection. Maintenance plan items control the maintenance and inspection tasks that are performed on maintenance objects. These items control when maintenance or inspection tasks are performed using maintenance cycles for which time and performance-based inspection intervals are defined. Depending on Customizing settings, as a maintenance plan is scheduled, maintenance calls are created and converted to orders when the calls are due. As an order is released, an inspection lot is created and the maintenance task list is selected and assigned to the maintenance plan. Each task list structure contains operations and possibly sub-operations that describe the work to be performed during a calibration inspection. Inspection characteristics that describe what will be inspected using quantitative or qualitative inspection specifications can be assigned to the task list. Following the selection and assignment of the task list, the calibration inspection operations are performed in chronological order and characteristic inspection

213

results are recorded and valuated. Next, based on the valuation of the inspection characteristics, a usage decision for the inspection lot is documented and the inspection lot is completed. The completion of the calibration inspection triggers an update to the test equipment status in the equipment master record to reflect the test equipment valuation as indicated by the lot's usage decision. In turn, the activities of the calibration inspection are confirmed for the maintenance order.

Q-118:   A. Inspection type and C. Order type

Test equipment is regularly inspected and calibrated to ensure that it adheres to predefined performance criteria is suitable for quality inspections. The results of the calibration inspection govern the release of the test equipment for subsequent use.   The planning, scheduling and performance of calibration inspections require the master data, as well as the planning and processing functions of the Test Equipment Management component. In particular, the functions required to plan a calibration inspection include the creation of an equipment master record, measuring points with reference to class characteristics and a maintenance strategy. Also required are the creation of a task list, an inspection lot, master inspection characteristics and a maintenance plan. In turn, Customizing requirements include the definition of an inspection type, inspection points, default values for the inspection type and an order type. Also required are the assignment of inspection types to the order types, materials to task list operations, objects to the

maintenance plan items and master inspection characteristics to operations.

Q-119:   A. Defines maintenance object and B. Defines maintenance task list

A maintenance plan is the central planning object for a calibration inspection. Maintenance plan items control the maintenance and inspection tasks that are performed on particular maintenance objects. These items use maintenance cycles for which time- and performance-based inspection intervals are defined to control when maintenance or inspection tasks are performed. Depending on Customizing settings, as a maintenance plan is scheduled, maintenance calls are created and converted to orders when the calls are due. As an order is released, an inspection lot is created and the maintenance task list is selected and assigned to the maintenance plan. Each task list structure contains operations and possibly sub-operations that describe the work to be performed during a calibration inspection. Inspection characteristics that describe what will be inspected using quantitative or qualitative inspection specifications can be assigned to the task list. Following the selection and assignment of the task list, the calibration inspection operations are performed in chronological order and characteristic inspection results are recorded and valuated. Next, based on the valuation of the inspection characteristics, a usage decision for the inspection lot is documented and the inspection lot is completed. The completion of the calibration inspection triggers an update to the test equipment status in the equipment master record to

reflect the test equipment valuation as indicated by the lot's usage decision. In turn, the activities of the calibration inspection are confirmed for the maintenance order.

Q-120: A. The use of both time- and performance-based maintenance cycles to determine maintenance dates for maintenance plan items

A maintenance plan is the central planning object for a calibration inspection. In particular, a multiple-counter plan refers to the use of both time and performance-based maintenance cycles to determine maintenance dates for maintenance plan items. Maintenance plan items control the maintenance and inspection tasks that are performed on maintenance objects. These items use maintenance cycles for which time and performance-based inspection intervals are defined to control when maintenance or inspection tasks are performed. Depending on Customizing settings, as a maintenance plan is scheduled, maintenance calls are created and converted to orders when the calls are due. As an order is released, an inspection lot is created and the maintenance task list is selected and assigned to the maintenance plan. Each task list contains both operations and sub-operations that describe the work to be performed during a calibration inspection. Inspection characteristics that describe what will be inspected using quantitative or qualitative inspection specifications can be assigned to the task list. Following the selection and assignment of the task list, the calibration inspection operations are performed in chronological order and characteristic inspection

results are recorded and valuated. Next, based on the valuation of the inspection characteristics, a usage decision for the inspection lot is documented and the inspection lot is completed. The completion of the calibration inspection triggers an update to the test equipment status in the equipment master record to reflect the test equipment valuation as indicated by the lot's usage decision. In turn, the activities of the calibration inspection are confirmed for the maintenance order.

Q-121:   A. Enables the creation of inspection lot when maintenance order is generated

Test equipment is regularly inspected and calibrated to ensure that it adheres to predefined performance criteria is suitable for quality inspections. The results of the calibration inspection govern the release of the test equipment for subsequent use. The planning, scheduling and performance of calibration inspections require the master data, as well as the planning and processing functions of the Test Equipment Management component. In particular, the functions required to plan a calibration inspection include the creation of an equipment master record, measuring points with reference to class characteristics and a maintenance strategy. Also required are the creation of a task list, an inspection lot, master inspection characteristics and a maintenance plan. In turn, Customizing requirements include the definition of an inspection type, inspection points, default values for the inspection type and an order type. Also required are the assignment of inspection types to the order types, materials to task list operations, objects to the maintenance plan items and master inspection characteristics to operations.

Q-122: A. Equipment master record

A usage decision code for an inspection lot documents the outcome of a calibration inspection and concludes the calibration inspection. On the basis of this code and its linkage to follow-up actions, individual functions can be performed automatically. One such follow-up function is the calculation of a quality score for the inspection lot. Other follow-up actions include using the cycle modification factor to update the inspection interval in the preventive maintenance plan and creating measurement documents for each measuring point to record inspection results. Additional follow-up actions include updating the status of a piece of equipment in the equipment master record to reflect the usage decision for the inspection and the technical completion of a maintenance order.

Q-123: A. Maintenance plan

A maintenance plan is the central planning object for a calibration inspection. Maintenance plan items control the maintenance and inspection tasks that are performed on maintenance objects. These items control when maintenance or inspection tasks are performed using maintenance cycles for which time and performance-based inspection intervals are defined. Depending on Customizing settings, as a maintenance plan is scheduled, maintenance calls are created and converted to orders when the calls are due. As an order is released, an inspection lot is created and the maintenance task list is selected and assigned to the maintenance plan. Each task list structure contains operations and possibly sub-operations that describe the work to be performed during a calibration inspection. Inspection characteristics that describe what will be inspected using quantitative or qualitative inspection specifications can be assigned to the task list. Following the selection and assignment of the task list, the calibration inspection operations are performed in chronological order and characteristic inspection results are recorded and valuated. Next, based on the valuation of the inspection characteristics, a usage decision for the inspection lot is documented and the inspection lot is completed. The completion of the calibration inspection triggers an update to the test equipment status in the equipment master record to reflect the test equipment valuation as indicated by the lot's usage decision. In turn, the activities of the calibration inspection are confirmed for the maintenance order.

Q-124: A. Time-based maintenance plan with maintenance strategy

A maintenance plan is the central planning object for a calibration inspection. For example, a time-based maintenance plan with a maintenance strategy can be used to implement a time-based maintenance cycle. Maintenance plan items control the maintenance and inspection tasks that are performed on maintenance objects. These items control when maintenance or inspection tasks are performed using maintenance cycles for which time and performance-based inspection intervals are defined. Depending on Customizing settings, as a maintenance plan is scheduled, maintenance calls are created and converted to orders when the calls are due. As an order is released, an inspection lot is created and the maintenance task list is selected and assigned to the maintenance plan. Each task list structure contains operations and possibly sub-operations that describe the work to be performed during a calibration inspection. Inspection characteristics that describe what will be inspected using quantitative or qualitative inspection specifications can be assigned to the task list. Following the selection and assignment of the task list, the calibration inspection operations are performed in chronological order and characteristic inspection results are recorded and valuated. Next, based on the valuation of the inspection characteristics, a usage decision for the inspection lot is documented and the inspection lot is completed. The completion of the calibration inspection triggers an update to the test equipment status in the equipment master record to reflect the test equipment valuation as indicated by the lot's usage decision. In turn, the activities of the calibration inspection are confirmed for the maintenance order.

Q-125:   A. Scheduling parameter, B. Task list and E. Maintenance plan category

Test equipment is regularly inspected and calibrated to ensure that it adheres to predefined performance criteria is suitable for quality inspections. The results of

the calibration inspection govern the release of the test equipment for subsequent use. The planning, scheduling and performance of calibration inspections require the master data, as well as the planning and processing functions of the Test Equipment Management component. In particular, the functions required to plan a calibration inspection include the creation of an equipment master record, measuring points with reference to class characteristics and a maintenance strategy. Also required are the creation of a task list, an inspection lot, master inspection characteristics and a maintenance plan. In turn, Customizing requirements include the definition of an inspection type, inspection points, default values for the inspection type and an order type. Also required are the assignment of inspection types to the order types, materials to task list operations, objects to the maintenance plan items and master inspection characteristics to operations.

Q-126:   B. Assign class characteristic to measuring point

A usage decision code for an inspection lot concludes an inspection and documents its outcome. On the basis of this code and its linkage to follow-up functions, the functions can be executed automatically. One such follow-up action is the creation of measurement documents to record inspection results for each inspection point that's defined for the test equipment. The critical values obtained by measurement readings are recorded in the documents and used to monitor a technical installation. The measurement documents are stored in the test equipment master record. The requirements for this functionality include the linkage of master inspection characteristics in the maintenance task list to measuring point master records by means of the class characteristics, as well as the creation of measuring point categories. Also required is the assignment of qualitative characteristics to the measuring point.

Q-127: B. Performance-based maintenance plan with maintenance strategy and E. Single-cycle performance-based maintenance plan

A maintenance plan is the central planning object for a calibration inspection. To ensure that test equipment is inspected and calibrated on the basis of use, a performance-based maintenance plan with maintenance strategy or single-cycle performance-based maintenance plan can be used. Maintenance plan items control the maintenance and inspection tasks that are performed on maintenance objects. These items control when maintenance or inspection tasks are performed using maintenance cycles for which time and performance-based inspection intervals are defined. Depending on Customizing settings, as a maintenance plan is scheduled, maintenance calls are created and converted to orders when the calls are due. As an order is released, an inspection lot is created and the maintenance task list is selected and assigned to the maintenance plan. Each task list structure contains operations and possibly sub-operations that describe the work to be performed during a calibration inspection. Inspection characteristics that describe

what will be inspected using quantitative or qualitative inspection specifications can be assigned to the task list. Following the selection and assignment of the task list, the calibration inspection operations are performed in chronological order and characteristic inspection results are recorded and valuated. Next, based on the valuation of the inspection characteristics, a usage decision for the inspection lot is documented and the inspection lot is completed. The completion of the calibration inspection triggers an update to the test equipment status in the equipment master record to reflect the test equipment valuation as indicated by the lot's usage decision. In turn, the activities of the calibration inspection are confirmed for the maintenance order.

Q-128:   A. Unit of measure for the maintenance cycle and C. Maintenance plan category

Test equipment is regularly inspected and calibrated to ensure that it adheres to predefined performance criteria is suitable for quality inspections. The results of the calibration inspection govern the release of the test equipment for subsequent use. The planning, scheduling and performance of calibration inspections require the master data, as well as the planning and processing functions of the Test Equipment Management component. In particular, the functions required to plan a calibration inspection include the creation of an equipment master record, measuring points with reference to class characteristics and a maintenance strategy. Also required are the creation of a task list, an inspection lot, master inspection characteristics and a maintenance plan. In turn, Customizing requirements include the definition of an inspection type, inspection points, default values for the inspection type and an order type. Also required are the assignment of inspection types to the order types, materials to task list operations, objects to the maintenance plan items and master inspection characteristics to operations.

Q-129: A. Creation of master inspection characteristic, C. Creation of task list and E. Creation of maintenance plan

Test equipment is regularly inspected and calibrated to ensure that it adheres to predefined performance criteria is suitable for quality inspections. The results of the calibration inspection govern the release of the test equipment for subsequent use. The planning, scheduling and performance of calibration inspections require the master data, as well as the planning and processing functions of the Test Equipment Management component. In particular, the functions required to plan a calibration inspection include the creation of an equipment master record, measuring points with reference to class characteristics and a maintenance strategy. Also required are the creation of a task list, an inspection lot, master inspection characteristics and a maintenance plan. In turn, Customizing requirements include the definition of an inspection type, inspection points, default values for the inspection type and an order type. Also required are the assignment of inspection types to the order types, materials to task list operations, objects to the

maintenance plan items and master inspection characteristics to operations.

Q-130:   A. Maintenance plan

A maintenance plan is the central planning object for a calibration inspection. Maintenance plan items control the maintenance and inspection tasks that are performed on a particular maintenance object. These items use maintenance cycles for which time- and performance-based inspection intervals are defined to control when maintenance or inspection tasks are performed. Depending on Customizing settings, as a maintenance plan is scheduled, maintenance calls are created and converted to orders when the calls are due. As an order is released, an inspection lot is created and the maintenance task list is selected and assigned to the maintenance plan. Each task list structure contains operations and possibly sub-operations that describe the work to be performed during a calibration inspection. Inspection characteristics that describe what will be inspected using quantitative or qualitative inspection specifications can be assigned to the task list. Following the selection and assignment of the task list, the calibration inspection operations are performed in chronological order and characteristic inspection results are recorded and valuated. Next, based on the valuation of the inspection characteristics, a usage decision for the inspection lot is documented and the inspection lot is completed. The completion of the calibration inspection triggers an update to the test equipment status in the equipment master record to reflect the test equipment valuation as indicated by the

lot's usage decision. In turn, the activities of the calibration inspection are confirmed for the maintenance order.

Q-131:   D. All of the above

Test equipment is regularly inspected and calibrated to ensure that it adheres to predefined performance criteria is suitable for quality inspections. The results of the calibration inspection govern the release of the test equipment for subsequent use. The planning, scheduling and performance of calibration inspections require the master data, as well as the planning and processing functions of the Test Equipment Management component. In particular, the functions required to plan a calibration inspection include the creation of an equipment master record, measuring points with reference to class characteristics and a maintenance strategy. Also required are the creation of a task list, an inspection lot, master inspection characteristics and a maintenance plan. In turn, Customizing requirements include the definition of an inspection type, inspection points, default values for the inspection type and an order type. Also required are the assignment of inspection types to the order types, materials to task list operations, objects to the maintenance plan items and master inspection characteristics to operations.

Q-132:   A. Maintenance plan

A maintenance plan is the central planning object for a calibration inspection. Maintenance plan items control

the maintenance and inspection tasks that are performed on maintenance objects. These items control when maintenance or inspection tasks are performed using maintenance cycles for which time and performance-based inspection intervals are defined. Depending on Customizing settings, as a maintenance plan is scheduled, maintenance calls are created and converted to orders when the calls are due. As an order is released, an inspection lot is created and the maintenance task list is selected and assigned to the maintenance plan. Each task list structure contains operations and possibly sub-operations that describe the work to be performed during a calibration inspection. Inspection characteristics that describe what will be inspected using quantitative or qualitative inspection specifications can be assigned to the task list. Following the selection and assignment of the task list, the calibration inspection operations are performed in chronological order and characteristic inspection results are recorded and valuated. Next, based on the valuation of the inspection characteristics, a usage decision for the inspection lot is documented and the inspection lot is completed. The completion of the calibration inspection triggers an update to the test equipment status in the equipment master record to reflect the test equipment valuation as indicated by the lot's usage decision. In turn, the activities of the calibration inspection are confirmed for the maintenance order.

Q-133:   A. Create maintenance plan and C. Assign task list to maintenance plan

Test equipment is regularly inspected and calibrated to ensure that it adheres to predefined performance criteria is suitable for quality inspections. The results of the calibration inspection govern the release of the test equipment for subsequent use. The planning, scheduling and performance of calibration inspections require the master data, as well as the planning and processing functions of the Test Equipment Management component. In particular, the functions required to plan a calibration inspection include the creation of an equipment master record, measuring points with reference to class characteristics and a maintenance strategy. Also required are the creation of a task list, an inspection lot, master inspection characteristics and a maintenance plan. In turn, Customizing requirements include the definition of an inspection type, inspection points, default values for the inspection type and an order type. Also required are the assignment of inspection types to the order types, materials to task list operations, objects to the maintenance plan items and master inspection characteristics to operations.

Q-134: A. Maintenance cycles in maintenance plan

A maintenance plan is the central planning object for a calibration inspection. Maintenance plan items control the maintenance and inspection tasks that are performed on maintenance objects. These items control when maintenance or inspection tasks are performed using maintenance cycles for which time and performance-based inspection intervals are defined. Depending on Customizing settings, as a maintenance

plan is scheduled, maintenance calls are created and converted to orders when the calls are due. As an order is released, an inspection lot is created and the maintenance task list is selected and assigned to the maintenance plan. Each task list structure contains operations and possibly sub-operations that describe the work to be performed during a calibration inspection. Inspection characteristics that describe what will be inspected using quantitative or qualitative inspection specifications can be assigned to the task list. Following the selection and assignment of the task list, the calibration inspection operations are performed in chronological order and characteristic inspection results are recorded and valuated. Next, based on the valuation of the inspection characteristics, a usage decision for the inspection lot is documented and the inspection lot is completed. The completion of the calibration inspection triggers an update to the test equipment status in the equipment master record to reflect the test equipment valuation as indicated by the lot's usage decision. In turn, the activities of the calibration inspection are confirmed for the maintenance order.

Q-135:   B. Enter maintenance plan category

Test equipment is regularly inspected and calibrated to ensure that it adheres to predefined performance criteria is suitable for quality inspections. The results of the calibration inspection govern the release of the test equipment for subsequent use. The planning, scheduling and performance of calibration inspections require the master data, as well as the planning and processing functions of the Test Equipment Management component. In particular, the functions required to plan a calibration inspection include the creation of an equipment master record, measuring points with reference to class characteristics and a maintenance strategy. Also required are the creation of a task list, an inspection lot, master inspection characteristics and a maintenance plan. In turn, Customizing requirements include the definition of an inspection type, inspection points, default values for the inspection type and an order type. Also required are the assignment of inspection types to the order types, materials to task list operations, objects to the maintenance plan items and master inspection characteristics to operations.

Q-136:   A. Performance-based maintenance plan

A maintenance plan is the central planning object for a calibration inspection. For example, to ensure that a calibration inspection is triggered by a series of measuring points, a performance-based maintenance plan is used. Maintenance plan items control the maintenance and inspection tasks that are performed on maintenance objects. These items control when maintenance or inspection tasks are performed using maintenance cycles for which time and performance-based inspection intervals are defined. Depending on Customizing settings, as a maintenance plan is scheduled, maintenance calls are created and converted to orders when the calls are due. As an order is released, an inspection lot is created and the maintenance task list is selected and assigned to the maintenance plan. Each task list structure contains

operations and possibly sub-operations that describe the work to be performed during a calibration inspection. Inspection characteristics that describe what will be inspected using quantitative or qualitative inspection specifications can be assigned to the task list. Following the selection and assignment of the task list, the calibration inspection operations are performed in chronological order and characteristic inspection results are recorded and valuated. Next, based on the valuation of the inspection characteristics, a usage decision for the inspection lot is documented and the inspection lot is completed. The completion of the calibration inspection triggers an update to the test equipment status in the equipment master record to reflect the test equipment valuation as indicated by the lot's usage decision. In turn, the activities of the calibration inspection are confirmed for the maintenance order.

Q-137:   B. Maintenance plan

A maintenance plan is the central planning object for a calibration inspection. Maintenance plan items control the maintenance and inspection tasks that are performed on maintenance objects. These items control when maintenance or inspection tasks are performed using maintenance cycles for which time and performance-based inspection intervals are defined. Depending on Customizing settings, as a maintenance plan is scheduled, maintenance calls are created and converted to orders when the calls are due. As an order is released, an inspection lot is created and the maintenance task list is selected and assigned to the

maintenance plan. Each task list structure contains operations and possibly sub-operations that describe the work to be performed during a calibration inspection. Inspection characteristics that describe what will be inspected using quantitative or qualitative inspection specifications can be assigned to the task list. Following the selection and assignment of the task list, the calibration inspection operations are performed in chronological order and characteristic inspection results are recorded and valuated. Next, based on the valuation of the inspection characteristics, a usage decision for the inspection lot is documented and the inspection lot is completed. The completion of the calibration inspection triggers an update to the test equipment status in the equipment master record to reflect the test equipment valuation as indicated by the lot's usage decision. In turn, the activities of the calibration inspection are confirmed for the maintenance order.

Q-138: A. Identifies maintenance object that's the subject of the maintenance tasks and C. Consists of maintenance items for which the maintenance objects and maintenance task list are defined

A maintenance plan is the central planning object for a calibration inspection. Maintenance plan items control the maintenance and inspection tasks that are performed on maintenance objects. These items control when maintenance or inspection tasks are performed using maintenance cycles for which time and performance-based inspection intervals are defined. Depending on Customizing settings, as a maintenance

plan is scheduled, maintenance calls are created and converted to orders when the calls are due. As an order is released, an inspection lot is created and the maintenance task list is selected and assigned to the maintenance plan. Each task list structure contains operations and possibly sub-operations that describe the work to be performed during a calibration inspection. Inspection characteristics that describe what will be inspected using quantitative or qualitative inspection specifications can be assigned to the task list. Following the selection and assignment of the task list, the calibration inspection operations are performed in chronological order and characteristic inspection results are recorded and valuated. Next, based on the valuation of the inspection characteristics, a usage decision for the inspection lot is documented and the inspection lot is completed. The completion of the calibration inspection triggers an update to the test equipment status in the equipment master record to reflect the test equipment valuation as indicated by the lot's usage decision. In turn, the activities of the calibration inspection are confirmed for the maintenance order.

Q-139:   A. Maintenance order

A maintenance plan is the central planning object for a calibration inspection. Maintenance plan items control the maintenance and inspection tasks that are performed on maintenance objects. These items control when maintenance or inspection tasks are performed using maintenance cycles for which time and performance-based inspection intervals are defined.

Depending on Customizing settings, as a maintenance plan is scheduled, maintenance calls are created and converted to orders when the calls are due. As an order is released, an inspection lot is created and the maintenance task list – equipment, functional or general task list -- is selected and assigned to the maintenance plan. Each task list structure contains operations and possibly sub-operations that describe the work to be performed during a calibration inspection. Inspection characteristics that describe what will be inspected using quantitative or qualitative inspection specifications can be assigned to the task list. Following the selection and assignment of the task list, the calibration inspection operations are performed in chronological order and characteristic inspection results are recorded and valuated. Next, based on the valuation of the inspection characteristics, a usage decision for the inspection lot is documented and the inspection lot is completed. The completion of the calibration inspection triggers an update to the test equipment status in the equipment master record to reflect the test equipment valuation as indicated by the lot's usage decision. In turn, the activities of the calibration inspection are confirmed for the maintenance order.

Q-140:   A. Time-based maintenance plan with maintenance strategy

A maintenance plan is the central planning object for a calibration inspection. Maintenance plan items control the maintenance and inspection tasks that are performed on maintenance objects. These items control when maintenance or inspection tasks are

performed using maintenance cycles for which time and performance-based inspection intervals are defined. Depending on Customizing settings, as a maintenance plan is scheduled, maintenance calls are created and converted to orders when the calls are due. As an order is released, an inspection lot is created and the maintenance task list – equipment, functional or general task list -- is selected and assigned to the maintenance plan. Each task list structure contains operations and possibly sub-operations that describe the work to be performed during a calibration inspection. Inspection characteristics that describe what will be inspected using quantitative or qualitative inspection specifications can be assigned to the task list. Following the selection and assignment of the task list, the calibration inspection operations are performed in chronological order and characteristic inspection results are recorded and valuated. Next, based on the valuation of the inspection characteristics, a usage decision for the inspection lot is documented and the inspection lot is completed. The completion of the calibration inspection triggers an update to the test equipment status in the equipment master record to reflect the test equipment valuation as indicated by the lot's usage decision. In turn, the activities of the calibration inspection are confirmed for the maintenance order.

Q-141:   B. Calibration inspection follow-up function

A usage decision code for an inspection lot documents the outcome of a calibration inspection and concludes the calibration inspection. On the basis of this code and its linkage to follow-up actions, individual functions can be performed automatically. One such follow-up function is the calculation of a quality score for the inspection lot. Other follow-up actions include using the cycle modification factor to update the inspection interval in the preventive maintenance plan and creating measurement documents for each measuring point to record inspection results. Additional follow-up actions include updating the status of a piece of equipment in the equipment master record to reflect the usage decision for the inspection and the technical completion of a maintenance order.

Q-142:   A. Maintenance item in maintenance plan

A maintenance plan is the central planning object for a calibration inspection. Maintenance plan items control the maintenance and inspection tasks that are performed on maintenance objects. These items control when maintenance or inspection tasks are performed using maintenance cycles for which time and performance-based inspection intervals are defined. Depending on Customizing settings, as a maintenance plan is scheduled, maintenance calls are created and converted to orders when the calls are due. As an order is released, an inspection lot is created and the maintenance task list is selected and assigned to the maintenance plan. Each task list structure contains operations and possibly sub-operations that describe the work to be performed during a calibration inspection. Inspection characteristics that describe what will be inspected using quantitative or qualitative inspection specifications can be assigned to the task list. Following the selection and assignment of the task list, the calibration inspection operations are performed in chronological order and characteristic inspection results are recorded and valuated. Next, based on the valuation of the inspection characteristics, a usage decision for the inspection lot is documented and the inspection lot is completed. The completion of the calibration inspection triggers an update to the test equipment status in the equipment master record to reflect the test equipment valuation as indicated by the lot's usage decision. In turn, the activities of the calibration inspection are confirmed for the maintenance order.

Q-143:   A. Parameter used to define maintenance plan

A usage decision code for an inspection lot concludes an inspection and documents its outcome. On the basis of this code and its linkage to follow-up functions, the functions can be executed automatically. One such follow-up action is the creation of measurement documents to record inspection results for each inspection point that's defined for the test equipment. The critical values obtained by measurement readings are recorded in the documents and used to monitor a technical installation. The measurement documents are stored in the test equipment master record. The requirements for this functionality include the linkage of master inspection characteristics in the maintenance task list to measuring point master records by means of the class characteristics, as well as the creation of measuring point categories. Also required is the assignment of qualitative characteristics to the measuring point.

Q-144:   B. Maintenance plan

A maintenance plan, which consists of one or more A maintenance plan is the central planning object for a calibration inspection. Maintenance plan items control the maintenance and inspection tasks that are performed on maintenance objects. These items control when maintenance or inspection tasks are performed using maintenance cycles for which time and performance-based inspection intervals are defined. Depending on Customizing settings, as a maintenance plan is scheduled, maintenance calls are created and converted to orders when the calls are due. As an order is released, an inspection lot is created and the maintenance task list is selected and assigned to the maintenance plan. Each task list structure contains operations and possibly sub-operations that describe the work to be performed during a calibration inspection. Inspection characteristics that describe what will be inspected using quantitative or qualitative inspection specifications can be assigned to the task list. Following the selection and assignment of the task list, the calibration inspection operations are performed in chronological order and characteristic inspection results are recorded and valuated. Next, based on the valuation of the inspection characteristics, a usage decision for the inspection lot is documented and the inspection lot is completed. The completion of the calibration inspection triggers an update to the test equipment status in the equipment master record to reflect the test equipment valuation as indicated by the lot's usage decision. In turn, the activities of the calibration inspection are confirmed for the maintenance order.

Q-145:   C. Define the maintenance tasks to be performed on individual due dates

A maintenance plan is the central planning object for a calibration inspection. Maintenance plan items control the maintenance and inspection tasks that are performed on maintenance objects. These items control when maintenance or inspection tasks are performed using maintenance cycles for which time and performance-based inspection intervals are defined. Depending on Customizing settings, as a maintenance plan is scheduled, maintenance calls are created and converted to orders when the calls are due. As an order is released, an inspection lot is created and the maintenance task list – equipment, functional or general task list -- is selected and assigned to the maintenance plan. Each task list structure contains operations and possibly sub-operations that describe the work to be performed during a calibration inspection. Inspection characteristics that describe what will be inspected using quantitative or qualitative inspection specifications can be assigned to the task list. Following the selection and assignment of the task list, the calibration inspection operations are performed in chronological order and characteristic inspection results are recorded and valuated. Next, based on the valuation of the inspection characteristics, a usage decision for the inspection lot is documented and the inspection lot is completed. The completion of the calibration inspection triggers an update to the test equipment status in the equipment master record to reflect the test equipment valuation as indicated by the lot's usage decision. In turn, the activities of the calibration inspection are confirmed for the maintenance order.

Q-146:   D. All of the above

A maintenance plan is the central planning object for a calibration inspection. Five types of maintenance plans are available. A maintenance plan with a maintenance strategy is time or performance-based. In turn, a maintenance plan without a maintenance strategy is a single-cycle time-based plan, a single-cycle performance-based plan or a multiple counter plan, which is time and performance-based. Maintenance plan items control the maintenance and inspection tasks that are performed on maintenance objects. These items control when maintenance or inspection tasks are performed using maintenance cycles for which time and performance-based inspection intervals are defined. Depending on Customizing settings, as a maintenance plan is scheduled, maintenance calls are created and converted to orders when the calls are due. As an order is released, an inspection lot is created and the maintenance task list is selected and assigned to the maintenance plan. Each task list structure contains operations and possibly sub-operations that describe the work to be performed during a calibration inspection. Inspection characteristics that describe what will be inspected using quantitative or qualitative inspection specifications can be assigned to the task list. Following the selection and assignment of the task list, the calibration inspection operations are performed in chronological order and characteristic inspection results are recorded and valuated. Next, based on the valuation of the inspection characteristics, a usage decision for the inspection lot is documented and the inspection lot is completed. The completion of the calibration inspection triggers an update to the test equipment status in the equipment master record to reflect the test equipment valuation as indicated by the lot's usage decision. In turn, the activities of the calibration inspection are confirmed for the maintenance order.

Q-147:   C. Equipment master record

A usage decision code for an inspection lot documents the outcome of a calibration inspection and concludes the calibration inspection. On the basis of this code and its linkage to follow-up actions, individual functions can be performed automatically. One such follow-up function is the calculation of a quality score for the inspection lot. Other follow-up actions include using the cycle modification factor to update the inspection interval in the preventive maintenance plan and creating measurement documents for each measuring point to record inspection results. Additional follow-up actions include updating the status of a piece of equipment in the equipment master record to reflect the usage decision for the inspection and the technical completion of a maintenance order.

Q-148: A. Maintenance plan

A maintenance plan is the central planning object for a calibration inspection. Maintenance plan items control the maintenance and inspection tasks that are performed on maintenance objects. These items control when maintenance or inspection tasks are performed using maintenance cycles for which time and performance-based inspection intervals are defined. Depending on Customizing settings, as a maintenance plan is scheduled, maintenance calls are created and converted to orders when the calls are due. As an order is released, an inspection lot is created and the maintenance task list is selected and assigned to the maintenance plan. Each task list structure contains operations and possibly sub-operations that describe the work to be performed during a calibration inspection. Inspection characteristics that describe what will be inspected using quantitative or qualitative inspection specifications can be assigned to the task list. Following the selection and assignment of the task list, the calibration inspection operations are performed in chronological order and characteristic inspection results are recorded and valuated. Next, based on the valuation of the inspection characteristics, a usage decision for the inspection lot is documented and the inspection lot is completed. The completion of the calibration inspection triggers an update to the test equipment status in the equipment master record to reflect the test equipment valuation as indicated by the lot's usage decision. In turn, the activities of the calibration inspection are confirmed for the maintenance order.

Q-149:   B. Maintenance plan

A maintenance plan is the central planning object for a calibration inspection. Maintenance plan items control the maintenance and inspection tasks that are performed on maintenance objects. These items control when maintenance or inspection tasks are performed using maintenance cycles for which time and performance-based inspection intervals are defined. Depending on Customizing settings, as a maintenance plan is scheduled, maintenance calls are created and converted to orders when the calls are due. As an order is released, an inspection lot is created and the maintenance task list is selected and assigned to the maintenance plan. Each task list structure contains operations and possibly sub-operations that describe the work to be performed during a calibration inspection. Inspection characteristics that describe what will be inspected using quantitative or qualitative inspection specifications can be assigned to the task list. Following the selection and assignment of the task list, the calibration inspection operations are performed in chronological order and characteristic inspection results are recorded and valuated. Next, based on the valuation of the inspection characteristics, a usage decision for the inspection lot is documented and the inspection lot is completed. The completion of the calibration inspection triggers an update to the test equipment status in the equipment master record to reflect the test equipment valuation as indicated by the lot's usage decision. In turn, the activities of the calibration inspection are confirmed for the maintenance order.

Q-150:   A. Time-based maintenance plan with maintenance strategy, B. Performance-based maintenance plan with maintenance strategy and D. Time-based single cycle maintenance plan

A maintenance plan is the central planning object for a calibration inspection. Five types of maintenance plans are available. A maintenance plan with a maintenance strategy is time or performance-based. In turn, a maintenance plan without a maintenance strategy is a single-cycle time-based plan, a single-cycle performance-based plan or a multiple counter plan, which is time and performance-based. Maintenance plan items control the maintenance and inspection tasks that are performed on maintenance objects. These items control when maintenance or inspection tasks are performed using maintenance cycles for which time and performance-based inspection intervals are defined. Depending on Customizing settings, as a maintenance plan is scheduled, maintenance calls are created and converted to orders when the calls are due. As an order is released, an inspection lot is created and the maintenance task list is selected and assigned to the maintenance plan. Each task list structure contains operations and possibly sub-operations that describe the work to be performed during a calibration inspection. Inspection characteristics that describe what will be inspected using quantitative or qualitative inspection specifications can be assigned to the task list. Following the selection and assignment of the task list, the calibration inspection operations are performed in chronological order and characteristic inspection results are recorded and valuated. Next, based on the valuation of the inspection characteristics, a usage decision for the inspection lot is documented and the inspection lot is completed. The completion of the calibration inspection triggers an update to the test equipment status in the equipment master record to reflect the test equipment valuation as indicated by the lot's usage decision. In turn, the activities of the calibration inspection are confirmed for the maintenance order.

Q-151:   A. Maintenance plan not defined

Test equipment is regularly inspected and calibrated to ensure that it adheres to predefined performance criteria is suitable for quality inspections. The results of the calibration inspection govern the release of the test equipment for subsequent use. The planning, scheduling and performance of calibration inspections require the master data, as well as the planning and processing functions of the Test Equipment Management component. In particular, the functions required to plan a calibration inspection include the creation of an equipment master record, measuring points with reference to class characteristics and a maintenance strategy. Also required are the creation of a task list, an inspection lot, master inspection characteristics and a maintenance plan. In turn, Customizing requirements include the definition of an inspection type, inspection points, default values for the inspection type and an order type. Also required are the assignment of inspection types to the order types, materials to task list operations, objects to the

maintenance plan items and master inspection characteristics to operations.

Q-152:   A. Maintenance plan with maintenance strategy and B. Single cycle plan

A maintenance plan is the central planning object for a calibration inspection. For example, maintenance plans that are structured in reference to time include a single-cycle plan and a maintenance plan with a maintenance strategy. Maintenance plan items control the maintenance and inspection tasks that are performed on maintenance objects. These items control when maintenance or inspection tasks are performed using maintenance cycles for which time and performance-based inspection intervals are defined. Depending on Customizing settings, as a maintenance plan is scheduled, maintenance calls are created and converted to orders when the calls are due. As an order is released, an inspection lot is created and the maintenance task list is selected and assigned to the maintenance plan. Each task list structure contains operations and possibly sub-operations that describe the work to be performed during a calibration inspection. Inspection characteristics that describe what will be inspected using quantitative or qualitative inspection specifications can be assigned to the task list. Following the selection and assignment of the task list, the calibration inspection operations are performed in chronological order and characteristic inspection results are recorded and valuated. Next, based on the valuation of the inspection characteristics, a usage decision for the inspection lot is documented and the inspection lot is completed. The completion of the calibration inspection triggers an update to the test equipment status in the equipment master record to reflect the test equipment valuation as indicated by the lot's usage decision. In turn, the activities of the calibration inspection are confirmed for the maintenance order.

Q-153:   A. Measure the wear rate to a piece of test equipment and B. Input to performance-based maintenance plan

A usage decision code for an inspection lot concludes an inspection and documents its outcome. On the basis of this code and its linkage to follow-up functions, the functions can be executed automatically. One such follow-up action is the creation of measurement documents to record inspection results for each inspection point that's defined for the test equipment. The critical values obtained by measurement readings are recorded in the documents and used to monitor a technical installation. The measurement documents are stored in the test equipment master record. The requirements for this functionality include the linkage of master inspection characteristics in the maintenance task list to measuring point master records by means of the class characteristics, as well as the creation of measuring point categories. Also required is the assignment of qualitative characteristics to the measuring point.

Q-154:   A. PM05

Test equipment is regularly inspected and calibrated to ensure that it adheres to predefined performance criteria is suitable for quality inspections. The results of the calibration inspection govern the release of the test equipment for subsequent use. The planning, scheduling and performance of calibration inspections require the master data, as well as the planning and processing functions of the Test Equipment Management component. In particular, the functions required to plan a calibration inspection include the creation of an equipment master record, measuring points with reference to class characteristics and a maintenance strategy. Also required are the creation of a task list, an inspection lot, master inspection characteristics and a maintenance plan. In turn, Customizing requirements include the definition of an inspection type, inspection points, default values for the inspection type and an order type. Also required are the assignment of inspection type PM05 to the order type, materials to task list operations, objects to the maintenance plan items and master inspection characteristics to operations.

Q-155:   A. Determines the tasks to be performed on a due date

A maintenance plan is the central planning object for a calibration inspection. Maintenance plan items control the maintenance and inspection tasks that are performed on maintenance objects. These items control when maintenance or inspection tasks are performed using maintenance cycles for which time and performance-based inspection intervals are defined. Depending on Customizing settings, as a maintenance

248

plan is scheduled, maintenance calls are created and converted to orders when the calls are due. As an order is released, an inspection lot is created and the maintenance task list is selected and assigned to the maintenance plan. Each task list structure contains operations and possibly sub-operations that describe the work to be performed during a calibration inspection. Inspection characteristics that describe what will be inspected using quantitative or qualitative inspection specifications can be assigned to the task list. Following the selection and assignment of the task list, the calibration inspection operations are performed in chronological order and characteristic inspection results are recorded and valuated. Next, based on the valuation of the inspection characteristics, a usage decision for the inspection lot is documented and the inspection lot is completed. The completion of the calibration inspection triggers an update to the test equipment status in the equipment master record to reflect the test equipment valuation as indicated by the lot's usage decision. In turn, the activities of the calibration inspection are confirmed for the maintenance order.

Q-156:   B. Creation of maintenance plan and D. Creation of task list

Test equipment is regularly inspected and calibrated to ensure that it adheres to predefined performance criteria is suitable for quality inspections. The results of the calibration inspection govern the release of the test equipment for subsequent use. The planning, scheduling and performance of calibration inspections require the master data, as well as the planning and processing functions of the Test Equipment Management component. In particular, the functions required to plan a calibration inspection include the creation of an equipment master record, measuring points with reference to class characteristics and a maintenance strategy. Also required are the creation of a task list, an inspection lot, master inspection characteristics and a maintenance plan. In turn, Customizing requirements include the definition of an inspection type, inspection points, default values for the inspection type and an order type. Also required are the assignment of inspection type PM05 to the order type, materials to task list operations, objects to the maintenance plan items and master inspection characteristics to operations.

Q-157:   A. Maintenance plan with maintenance strategy

A maintenance plan is the central planning object for a calibration inspection. Maintenance plan items control the maintenance and inspection tasks that are performed on maintenance objects. These items control when maintenance or inspection tasks are performed using maintenance cycles for which time and performance-based inspection intervals are defined. Depending on Customizing settings, as a maintenance plan is scheduled, maintenance calls are created and converted to orders when the calls are due. As an order is released, an inspection lot is created and the maintenance task list is selected and assigned to the maintenance plan. Each task list structure contains

operations and possibly sub-operations that describe the work to be performed during a calibration inspection. Inspection characteristics that describe what will be inspected using quantitative or qualitative inspection specifications can be assigned to the task list. Following the selection and assignment of the task list, the calibration inspection operations are performed in chronological order and characteristic inspection results are recorded and valuated. Next, based on the valuation of the inspection characteristics, a usage decision for the inspection lot is documented and the inspection lot is completed. The completion of the calibration inspection triggers an update to the test equipment status in the equipment master record to reflect the test equipment valuation as indicated by the lot's usage decision. In turn, the activities of the calibration inspection are confirmed for the maintenance order.

Q-158:   A. Performance-based maintenance plan with maintenance strategy

A maintenance plan is the central planning object for a calibration inspection. A maintenance plan with a maintenance strategy may be time or performance-based. Maintenance plan items control the maintenance and inspection tasks that are performed on maintenance objects. These items control when maintenance or inspection tasks are performed using maintenance cycles for which time and performance-based inspection intervals are defined. Depending on Customizing settings, as a maintenance plan is scheduled, maintenance calls are created and converted to orders when the calls are due. As an order is released, an inspection lot is created and the maintenance task list is selected and assigned to the maintenance plan. Each task list structure contains operations and possibly sub-operations that describe the work to be performed during a calibration inspection. Inspection characteristics that describe what will be inspected using quantitative or qualitative inspection specifications can be assigned to the task list. Following the selection and assignment of the task list, the calibration inspection operations are performed in chronological order and characteristic inspection results are recorded and valuated. Next, based on the valuation of the inspection characteristics, a usage decision for the inspection lot is documented and the inspection lot is completed. The completion of the calibration inspection triggers an update to the test equipment status in the equipment master record to reflect the test equipment valuation as indicated by the lot's usage decision. In turn, the activities of the calibration inspection are confirmed for the maintenance order.

Q-159:   B. Maintenance plan

A maintenance plan is the central planning object for a calibration inspection. Maintenance plan items control the maintenance and inspection tasks that are performed on maintenance objects. These items control when maintenance or inspection tasks are performed using maintenance cycles for which time and performance-based inspection intervals are defined. Depending on Customizing settings, as a maintenance

plan is scheduled, maintenance calls are created and converted to orders when the calls are due. As an order is released, an inspection lot is created and the maintenance task list is selected and assigned to the maintenance plan. Each task list structure contains operations and possibly sub-operations that describe the work to be performed during a calibration inspection. Inspection characteristics that describe what will be inspected using quantitative or qualitative inspection specifications can be assigned to the task list. Following the selection and assignment of the task list, the calibration inspection operations are performed in chronological order and characteristic inspection results are recorded and valuated. Next, based on the valuation of the inspection characteristics, a usage decision for the inspection lot is documented and the inspection lot is completed. The completion of the calibration inspection triggers an update to the test equipment status in the equipment master record to reflect the test equipment valuation as indicated by the lot's usage decision. In turn, the activities of the calibration inspection are confirmed for the maintenance order.

Q-160: B. Maintenance plan

A maintenance plan is the central planning object for a calibration inspection. Maintenance plan items control the maintenance and inspection tasks that are performed on maintenance objects. These items control when maintenance or inspection tasks are performed using maintenance cycles for which time and performance-based inspection intervals are defined.

Depending on Customizing settings, as a maintenance plan is scheduled, maintenance calls are created and converted to orders when the calls are due. As an order is released, an inspection lot is created and the maintenance task list is selected and assigned to the maintenance plan. Each task list structure contains operations and possibly sub-operations that describe the work to be performed during a calibration inspection. Inspection characteristics that describe what will be inspected using quantitative or qualitative inspection specifications can be assigned to the task list. Following the selection and assignment of the task list, the calibration inspection operations are performed in chronological order and characteristic inspection results are recorded and valuated. Next, based on the valuation of the inspection characteristics, a usage decision for the inspection lot is documented and the inspection lot is completed. The completion of the calibration inspection triggers an update to the test equipment status in the equipment master record to reflect the test equipment valuation as indicated by the lot's usage decision. In turn, the activities of the calibration inspection are confirmed for the maintenance order.

Q-161:   A. Measuring point categories and B. Assignment of class characteristics to measuring points

A usage decision code for an inspection lot concludes an inspection and documents its outcome. On the basis of this code and its linkage to follow-up functions, the functions can be executed automatically. One such follow-up action is the creation of measurement documents to record inspection results for each inspection point that's defined for the test equipment. The critical values obtained by measurement readings are recorded in the documents and used to monitor a technical installation. The measurement documents are stored in the test equipment master record. The requirements for this functionality include the linkage of master inspection characteristics in the maintenance task list to measuring point master records by means of the class characteristics, as well as the creation of measuring point categories. Also required is the assignment of qualitative characteristics to the measuring point.

Q-162: A. Maintenance items

A maintenance plan is the central planning object for a calibration inspection. Maintenance plan items control the maintenance and inspection tasks that are performed on maintenance objects. These items control when maintenance or inspection tasks are performed using maintenance cycles for which time and performance-based inspection intervals are defined. Depending on Customizing settings, as a maintenance plan is scheduled, maintenance calls are created and converted to orders when the calls are due. As an order is released, an inspection lot is created and the maintenance task list is selected and assigned to the maintenance plan. Each task list structure contains operations and possibly sub-operations that describe the work to be performed during a calibration inspection. Inspection characteristics that describe what will be inspected using quantitative or qualitative inspection specifications can be assigned to the task list. Following the selection and assignment of the task list, the calibration inspection operations are performed in chronological order and characteristic inspection results are recorded and valuated. Next, based on the valuation of the inspection characteristics, a usage decision for the inspection lot is documented and the inspection lot is completed. The completion of the calibration inspection triggers an update to the test equipment status in the equipment master record to reflect the test equipment valuation as indicated by the lot's usage decision. In turn, the activities of the calibration inspection are confirmed for the maintenance order.

Q-163:   A. Equipment usage and C. Time schedule

A maintenance plan is the central planning object for a calibration inspection. Maintenance plan items control the maintenance and inspection tasks that are performed on maintenance objects. These items control when maintenance or inspection tasks are performed using maintenance cycles for which time and performance-based inspection intervals are defined. Depending on Customizing settings, as a maintenance plan is scheduled, maintenance calls are created and converted to orders when the calls are due. As an order is released, an inspection lot is created and the maintenance task list is selected and assigned to the maintenance plan. Each task list structure contains operations and possibly sub-operations that describe the work to be performed during a calibration inspection. Inspection characteristics that describe

what will be inspected using quantitative or qualitative inspection specifications can be assigned to the task list. Following the selection and assignment of the task list, the calibration inspection operations are performed in chronological order and characteristic inspection results are recorded and valuated. Next, based on the valuation of the inspection characteristics, a usage decision for the inspection lot is documented and the inspection lot is completed. The completion of the calibration inspection triggers an update to the test equipment status in the equipment master record to reflect the test equipment valuation as indicated by the lot's usage decision. In turn, the activities of the calibration inspection are confirmed for the maintenance order.

Q-164:   B. Create measuring point characteristic/counter with reference to class characteristic and C. Assign measuring point or counter to test equipment

A usage decision code for an inspection lot concludes an inspection and documents its outcome. On the basis of this code and its linkage to follow-up functions, the functions can be executed automatically. One such follow-up action is the creation of measurement documents to record inspection results for each inspection point that's defined for the test equipment. The critical values obtained by measurement readings are recorded in the documents and used to monitor a technical installation. The measurement documents are stored in the test equipment master record. The requirements for this functionality include the linkage of master inspection characteristics in the maintenance task list to measuring point master records by means of the class characteristics, as well as the creation of measuring point categories. Also required is the assignment of qualitative characteristics to the measuring point.

Q-165: B. Defines maintenance object and C. Defines maintenance task list

A maintenance plan is the central planning object for a calibration inspection. Maintenance plan items control the maintenance and inspection tasks that are performed on maintenance objects. These items control when maintenance or inspection tasks are performed using maintenance cycles for which time and performance-based inspection intervals are defined. Depending on Customizing settings, as a maintenance plan is scheduled, maintenance calls are created and converted to orders when the calls are due. As an order is released, an inspection lot is created and the maintenance task list is selected and assigned to the maintenance plan. Each task list structure contains operations and possibly sub-operations that describe the work to be performed during a calibration inspection. Inspection characteristics that describe what will be inspected using quantitative or qualitative inspection specifications can be assigned to the task list. Following the selection and assignment of the task list, the calibration inspection operations are performed in chronological order and characteristic inspection results are recorded and valuated. Next, based on the valuation of the inspection characteristics, a usage

decision for the inspection lot is documented and the inspection lot is completed. The completion of the calibration inspection triggers an update to the test equipment status in the equipment master record to reflect the test equipment valuation as indicated by the lot's usage decision. In turn, the activities of the calibration inspection are confirmed for the maintenance order.

Q-166:   A. Creation of maintenance or service order

A maintenance plan is the central planning object for a calibration inspection. Maintenance plan items control the maintenance and inspection tasks that are performed on maintenance objects. These items control when maintenance or inspection tasks are performed using maintenance cycles for which time and performance-based inspection intervals are defined. Depending on Customizing settings, as a maintenance plan is scheduled, maintenance calls are created and converted to orders when the calls are due. As an order is released, an inspection lot is created and the maintenance task list – equipment, functional or general -- is selected and assigned to the maintenance plan. Each task list structure contains operations and possibly sub-operations that describe the work to be performed during a calibration inspection. Inspection characteristics that describe what will be inspected using quantitative or qualitative inspection specifications can be assigned to the task list. Following the selection and assignment of the task list, the calibration inspection operations are performed in chronological order and characteristic inspection results are recorded and valuated. Next, based on the valuation of the inspection characteristics, a usage decision for the inspection lot is documented and the inspection lot is completed. The completion of the calibration inspection triggers an update to the test equipment status in the equipment master record to reflect the test equipment valuation as indicated by the lot's usage decision. In turn, the activities of the calibration inspection are confirmed for the maintenance order.

Q-167:   A. Order

A maintenance plan is the central planning object for a calibration inspection. Maintenance plan items control the maintenance and inspection tasks that are performed on maintenance objects. These items control when maintenance or inspection tasks are performed using maintenance cycles for which time and performance-based inspection intervals are defined. Depending on Customizing settings, as a maintenance plan is scheduled, maintenance calls are created and converted to orders when the calls are due. As an order is released, an inspection lot is created and the maintenance task list is selected and assigned to the maintenance plan. Each task list structure contains operations and possibly sub-operations that describe the work to be performed by internal or external parties during a calibration inspection. Inspection characteristics that describe what will be inspected using quantitative or qualitative inspection specifications can be assigned to the task list. Following the selection and assignment of the task list, the calibration inspection operations are performed in chronological order and characteristic inspection results are recorded and valuated. Next, based on the valuation of the inspection characteristics, a usage decision for the inspection lot is documented and the inspection lot is completed. The completion of the calibration inspection triggers an update to the test equipment status in the equipment master record to reflect the test equipment valuation as indicated by the lot's usage decision. In turn, the activities of the calibration inspection are confirmed for the maintenance order.

Q-168:   D. All of the above

A maintenance plan is the central planning object for a calibration inspection. Maintenance plan items control the maintenance and inspection tasks that are performed on maintenance objects. These items control when maintenance or inspection tasks are performed using maintenance cycles for which time and performance-based inspection intervals are defined. Depending on Customizing settings, as a maintenance plan is scheduled, maintenance calls are created and converted to orders when the calls are due. As an order is released, an inspection lot is created and the maintenance task list is selected and assigned to the maintenance plan. Each task list structure contains operations and possibly sub-operations that describe the work to be performed during a calibration inspection. Inspection characteristics that describe what will be inspected using quantitative or qualitative inspection specifications can be assigned to the task list. Following the selection and assignment of the task list, the calibration inspection operations are performed in chronological order and characteristic inspection results are recorded and valuated. Next, based on the valuation of the inspection characteristics, a usage decision for the inspection lot is documented and the inspection lot is completed. The completion of the calibration inspection triggers an update to the test equipment status in the equipment master record to reflect the test equipment valuation as indicated by the lot's usage decision. In turn, the activities of the calibration inspection are confirmed for the maintenance order.

Q-169: A. Operation to define the activity to be performed at a work center

A maintenance plan is the central planning object for a calibration inspection. Maintenance plan items control the maintenance and inspection tasks that are performed on maintenance objects. These items control when maintenance or inspection tasks are performed using maintenance cycles for which time and performance-based inspection intervals are defined. Depending on Customizing settings, as a maintenance plan is scheduled, maintenance calls are created and converted to orders when the calls are due. As an order is released, an inspection lot is created and the maintenance task list is selected and assigned to the maintenance plan. Each task list structure contains operations and possibly sub-operations that describe the work to be performed at particular work centers during a calibration inspection. Inspection characteristics that describe what will be inspected using quantitative or qualitative inspection specifications can be assigned to the task list. Following the selection and assignment of the task list, the calibration inspection operations are performed in chronological order and characteristic inspection results are recorded and valuated. Next, based on the valuation of the inspection characteristics, a usage decision for the inspection lot is documented and the inspection lot is completed. The completion of the calibration inspection triggers an update to the test equipment status in the equipment master record to reflect the test equipment valuation as indicated by the lot's usage decision. In turn, the activities of the calibration inspection are confirmed for the maintenance order.

Q-170:   A. Define measuring points to record results for piece of test equipment and C. Link master inspection characteristic to measuring points

A usage decision code for an inspection lot concludes an inspection and documents its outcome. On the basis of this code and its linkage to follow-up functions, the functions can be executed automatically. One such follow-up action is the creation of measurement documents to record inspection results for each inspection point that's defined for the test equipment. The critical values obtained by measurement readings are recorded in the documents and used to monitor a technical installation. The measurement documents are stored in the test equipment master record. The requirements for this functionality include the linkage of master inspection characteristics in the maintenance task list to measuring point master records by means of the class characteristics, as well as the creation of measuring point categories. Also required is the assignment of qualitative characteristics to the measuring point.

Q-171:   A. Assignment of measuring point to equipment master record and B. Creation of measuring point characteristic with reference to class characteristic

A usage decision code for an inspection lot concludes an inspection and documents its outcome. On the basis of this code and its linkage to follow-up functions, the functions can be executed automatically. One such follow-up action is the creation of measurement documents to record inspection results for each inspection point that's defined for the test equipment. The critical values obtained by measurement readings are recorded in the documents and used to monitor a technical installation. The measurement documents are stored in the test equipment master record. The requirements for this functionality include the linkage of master inspection characteristics in the maintenance task list to measuring point master records by means of the class characteristics, as well as the creation of measuring point categories. Also required is the assignment of qualitative characteristics to the measuring point.

Q–172:   C. Usage Decision

A usage decision code for an inspection lot concludes an inspection and documents its outcome. On the basis of this code and its linkage to follow-up functions, the functions can be executed automatically. One such follow-up action is the creation of measurement documents to record inspection results for each inspection point that's defined for the test equipment. The critical values obtained by measurement readings are recorded in the documents and used to monitor a technical installation. The measurement documents are stored in the test equipment master record. The requirements for this functionality include the linkage of master inspection characteristics in the maintenance task list to measuring point master records by means of the class characteristics, as well as the creation of measuring point categories. Also required is the assignment of qualitative characteristics to the measuring point.

Q-173:   A. Maintenance schedule

A maintenance plan is the central planning object for a calibration inspection. Maintenance plan items control the maintenance and inspection tasks that are performed on maintenance objects. These items control when maintenance or inspection tasks are performed using maintenance cycles for which time and performance-based inspection intervals are defined. Depending on Customizing settings, as a maintenance plan is scheduled, maintenance calls are created and converted to orders when the calls are due. As an order is released, an inspection lot is created and the maintenance task list is selected and assigned to the maintenance plan. Each task list structure contains operations and possibly sub-operations that describe the work to be performed during a calibration inspection. Inspection characteristics that describe

what will be inspected using quantitative or qualitative inspection specifications can be assigned to the task list. Following the selection and assignment of the task list, the calibration inspection operations are performed in chronological order and characteristic inspection results are recorded and valuated. Next, based on the valuation of the inspection characteristics, a usage decision for the inspection lot is documented and the inspection lot is completed. The completion of the calibration inspection triggers an update to the test equipment status in the equipment master record to reflect the test equipment valuation as indicated by the lot's usage decision. In turn, the activities of the calibration inspection are confirmed for the maintenance order.

Q-174: A. Time-based maintenance schedule and B. Performance-based maintenance schedule

A maintenance plan is the central planning object for a calibration inspection. Maintenance plan items control the maintenance and inspection tasks that are performed on maintenance objects. These items control when maintenance or inspection tasks are performed using maintenance cycles for which time and performance-based inspection intervals are defined. Depending on Customizing settings, as a maintenance plan is scheduled, maintenance calls are created and converted to orders when the calls are due. As an order is released, an inspection lot is created and the maintenance task list is selected and assigned to the maintenance plan. Each task list structure contains operations and possibly sub-operations that describe the work to be performed during a calibration inspection. Inspection characteristics that describe what will be inspected using quantitative or qualitative inspection specifications can be assigned to the task list. Following the selection and assignment of the task list, the calibration inspection operations are performed in chronological order and characteristic inspection results are recorded and valuated. Next, based on the valuation of the inspection characteristics, a usage decision for the inspection lot is documented and the inspection lot is completed. The completion of the calibration inspection triggers an update to the test equipment status in the equipment master record to reflect the test equipment valuation as indicated by the lot's usage decision. In turn, the activities of the calibration inspection are confirmed for the maintenance order.

Q-175: B. PM05

Test equipment is regularly inspected and calibrated to ensure that it adheres to predefined performance criteria is suitable for quality inspections. The results of the calibration inspection govern the release of the test equipment for subsequent use. The planning, scheduling and performance of calibration inspections require the master data, as well as the planning and processing functions of the Test Equipment Management component. In particular, the functions required to plan a calibration inspection include the creation of an equipment master record, measuring points with reference to class characteristics and a maintenance strategy. Also required are the creation of a task list, an inspection lot, master inspection characteristics and a maintenance plan. In turn, Customizing requirements include the definition of an inspection type, inspection points, default values for the inspection type and an order type. Also required are the assignment of inspection type PM05 to the order type, materials to task list operations, objects to the maintenance plan items and master inspection characteristics to operations.

Q-176: A. Assignment of qualitative characteristic with selected set to measuring point

A usage decision code for an inspection lot concludes an inspection and documents its outcome. On the basis of this code and its linkage to follow-up functions, the functions can be executed automatically. One such follow-up action is the creation of measurement documents to record inspection results for each inspection point that's defined for the test equipment. The critical values obtained by measurement readings are recorded in the documents and used to monitor a technical installation. The measurement documents are stored in the test equipment master record. The requirements for this functionality include the linkage of master inspection characteristics in the maintenance task list to measuring point master records by means of the class characteristics, as well as the creation of measuring point categories. Also required is the assignment of qualitative characteristics to the measuring point.

Q-177:   C. Assignment of measuring point or counter to equipment master record

A usage decision code for an inspection lot concludes an inspection and documents its outcome. On the basis of this code and its linkage to follow-up functions, the functions can be executed automatically. One such follow-up action is the creation of measurement documents to record inspection results for each inspection point that's defined for the test equipment. The critical values obtained by measurement readings are recorded in the documents and used to monitor a technical installation. The measurement documents are stored in the test equipment master record. The requirements for this functionality include the linkage of master inspection characteristics in the maintenance task list to measuring point master records by means of the class characteristics, as well as the creation of measuring point categories. Also required is the assignment of qualitative characteristics to the measuring point.

Q-178:   A. Maintenance plan category and B. Scheduling parameters for the maintenance plan

Test equipment is regularly inspected and calibrated to ensure that it adheres to predefined performance criteria is suitable for quality inspections. The results of the calibration inspection govern the release of the test equipment for subsequent use. The planning, scheduling and performance of calibration inspections require the master data, as well as the planning and processing functions of the Test Equipment

Management component. In particular, the functions required to plan a calibration inspection include the creation of an equipment master record, measuring points with reference to class characteristics and a maintenance strategy. Also required are the creation of a task list, an inspection lot, master inspection characteristics and a maintenance plan. In turn, Customizing requirements include the definition of an inspection type, inspection points, default values for the inspection type and an order type. Also required are the assignment of inspection type PM05 to the order type, materials to task list operations, objects to the maintenance plan items and master inspection characteristics to operations.

Q-179:   A. Assign task list to maintenance plan and C. Create equipment master record

Test equipment is regularly inspected and calibrated to ensure that it adheres to predefined performance criteria is suitable for quality inspections. The results of the calibration inspection govern the release of the test equipment for subsequent use. The planning, scheduling and performance of calibration inspections require the master data, as well as the planning and processing functions of the Test Equipment Management component. In particular, the functions required to plan a calibration inspection include the creation of an equipment master record, measuring points with reference to class characteristics and a maintenance strategy. Also required are the creation of a task list, an inspection lot, master inspection characteristics and a maintenance plan. In turn,

Customizing requirements include the definition of an inspection type, inspection points, default values for the inspection type and an order type. Also required are the assignment of inspection type PM05 to the order type, materials to task list operations, objects to the maintenance plan items and master inspection characteristics to operations.

Q-180:   B. Quality Management

A maintenance plan is the central planning object for a calibration inspection. Maintenance plan items control the maintenance and inspection tasks that are performed on maintenance objects. These items control when maintenance or inspection tasks are performed using maintenance cycles for which time and performance-based inspection intervals are defined. Depending on PM Customizing settings, as a maintenance plan is scheduled, maintenance calls are created and converted to orders when the calls are due. As an order is released, an inspection lot is created and the maintenance task list is selected and assigned to the maintenance plan. Each task list structure contains operations and possibly sub-operations that describe the work to be performed during a calibration inspection. Inspection characteristics that describe what will be inspected using quantitative or qualitative inspection specifications can be assigned to the task list. Following the selection and assignment of the task list, the calibration inspection operations are performed in chronological order and characteristic inspection results are recorded and valuated. Next, based on the valuation of the inspection characteristics, a usage decision for the inspection lot is documented and the inspection lot is completed. The completion of the calibration inspection triggers an update to the test equipment status in the equipment master record to reflect the test equipment valuation as indicated by the lot's usage decision. In turn, the activities of the calibration inspection are confirmed for the maintenance order.

Q-181:   B. Creation of inspection lot

A maintenance plan is the central planning object for a calibration inspection. Maintenance plan items control the maintenance and inspection tasks that are performed on maintenance objects. These items control when maintenance or inspection tasks are performed using maintenance cycles for which time and performance-based inspection intervals are defined. Depending on Customizing settings, as a maintenance plan is scheduled, maintenance calls are created and converted to orders when the calls are due. As an order is released, an inspection lot is created and the maintenance task list is selected and assigned to the maintenance plan. Each task list structure contains operations and possibly sub-operations that describe the work to be performed during a calibration inspection. Inspection characteristics that describe what will be inspected using quantitative or qualitative inspection specifications can be assigned to the task list. Following the selection and assignment of the task list, the calibration inspection operations are performed in chronological order and characteristic inspection results are recorded and valuated. Next, based on the valuation of the inspection characteristics, a usage

decision for the inspection lot is documented and the inspection lot is completed. The completion of the calibration inspection triggers an update to the test equipment status in the equipment master record to reflect the test equipment valuation as indicated by the lot's usage decision. In turn, the activities of the calibration inspection are confirmed for the maintenance order.

Q-182:   C. Confirmation of maintenance plan counter

A maintenance plan is the central planning object for a calibration inspection. Maintenance plan items control the maintenance and inspection tasks that are performed on maintenance objects. These items control when maintenance or inspection tasks are performed using maintenance cycles for which time and performance-based inspection intervals are defined. To revise the plan, the maintenance plan counter is confirmed. Depending on Customizing settings, as a maintenance plan is scheduled, maintenance calls are created and converted to orders when the calls are due. As an order is released, an inspection lot is created and the maintenance task list is selected and assigned to the maintenance plan. Each task list structure contains operations and possibly sub-operations that describe the work to be performed during a calibration inspection. Inspection characteristics that describe what will be inspected using quantitative or qualitative inspection specifications can be assigned to the task list. Following the selection and assignment of the task list, the calibration inspection operations are performed in chronological order and characteristic inspection

results are recorded and valuated. Next, based on the valuation of the inspection characteristics, a usage decision for the inspection lot is documented and the inspection lot is completed. The completion of the calibration inspection triggers an update to the test equipment status in the equipment master record to reflect the test equipment valuation as indicated by the lot's usage decision. In turn, the activities of the calibration inspection are confirmed for the maintenance order.

Q-183:   A. Measure depreciation of test equipment

A usage decision code for an inspection lot concludes an inspection and documents its outcome. On the basis of this code and its linkage to follow-up functions, the functions can be executed automatically. One such follow-up action is the creation of measurement documents to record inspection results for each inspection point that's defined for the test equipment. The critical values obtained by measurement readings are recorded in the documents and used to monitor a technical installation. The measurement documents are stored in the test equipment master record. The requirements for this functionality include the linkage of master inspection characteristics in the maintenance task list to measuring point master records by means of the class characteristics, as well as the creation of measuring point categories. Also required is the assignment of qualitative characteristics to the measuring point.

Q-184:   A. Maintenance object and C. Maintenance task list

A maintenance plan is the central planning object for a calibration inspection. Maintenance plan items control the maintenance and inspection tasks that are performed on maintenance objects. These items control when maintenance or inspection tasks are performed using maintenance cycles for which time and performance-based inspection intervals are defined. Depending on Customizing settings, as a maintenance plan is scheduled, maintenance calls are created and converted to orders when the calls are due. As an order is released, an inspection lot is created and the maintenance task list is selected and assigned to the maintenance plan. Each task list structure contains operations and possibly sub-operations that describe the work to be performed during a calibration inspection. Inspection characteristics that describe what will be inspected using quantitative or qualitative inspection specifications can be assigned to the task list. Following the selection and assignment of the task list, the calibration inspection operations are performed in chronological order and characteristic inspection results are recorded and valuated. Next, based on the valuation of the inspection characteristics, a usage decision for the inspection lot is documented and the inspection lot is completed. The completion of the calibration inspection triggers an update to the test equipment status in the equipment master record to reflect the test equipment valuation as indicated by the lot's usage decision. In turn, the activities of the calibration inspection are confirmed for the maintenance order.

Q-185:   A. Assign inspection type to maintenance order type

Test equipment is regularly inspected and calibrated to ensure that it adheres to predefined performance criteria is suitable for quality inspections. The results of the calibration inspection govern the release of the test equipment for subsequent use. The planning, scheduling and performance of calibration inspections require the master data, as well as the planning and processing functions of the Test Equipment Management component. In particular, the functions required to plan a calibration inspection include the creation of an equipment master record, measuring points with reference to class characteristics and a maintenance strategy. Also required are the creation of a task list, an inspection lot, master inspection characteristics and a maintenance plan. In turn, Customizing requirements include the definition of an inspection type, inspection points, default values for the inspection type and an order type. Also required are the assignment of inspection type PM05 to the order type, materials to task list operations, objects to the maintenance plan items and master inspection characteristics to operations.

Q-186:   B. Maintenance task list

A maintenance plan is the central planning object for a calibration inspection. Maintenance plan items control the maintenance and inspection tasks that are performed on maintenance objects. These items control when maintenance or inspection tasks are

performed using maintenance cycles for which time and performance-based inspection intervals are defined. Depending on Customizing settings, as a maintenance plan is scheduled, maintenance calls are created and converted to orders when the calls are due. As an order is released, an inspection lot is created and the maintenance task list – equipment, functional or general task list -- is selected and assigned to the maintenance plan. Each task list structure contains operations and possibly sub-operations that describe the work to be performed during a calibration inspection. Inspection characteristics that describe what will be inspected using quantitative or qualitative inspection specifications can be assigned to the task list. Following the selection and assignment of the task list, the calibration inspection operations are performed in chronological order and characteristic inspection results are recorded and valuated. Next, based on the valuation of the inspection characteristics, a usage decision for the inspection lot is documented and the inspection lot is completed. The completion of the calibration inspection triggers an update to the test equipment status in the equipment master record to reflect the test equipment valuation as indicated by the lot's usage decision. In turn, the activities of the calibration inspection are confirmed for the maintenance order.

Q-187:   B. Maintenance task list

A maintenance plan is the central planning object for a calibration inspection. Maintenance plan items control the maintenance and inspection tasks that are performed on maintenance objects. These items control when maintenance or inspection tasks are

performed using maintenance cycles for which time and performance-based inspection intervals are defined. Depending on Customizing settings, as a maintenance plan is scheduled, maintenance calls are created and converted to orders when the calls are due. As an order is released, an inspection lot is created and the maintenance task list – equipment, functional or general task list -- is selected and assigned to the maintenance plan. Each task list structure contains operations and possibly sub-operations that describe the work to be performed during a calibration inspection. Inspection characteristics that describe what will be inspected using quantitative or qualitative inspection specifications can be assigned to the task list. Following the selection and assignment of the task list, the calibration inspection operations are performed in chronological order and characteristic inspection results are recorded and valuated. Next, based on the valuation of the inspection characteristics, a usage decision for the inspection lot is documented and the inspection lot is completed. The completion of the calibration inspection triggers an update to the test equipment status in the equipment master record to reflect the test equipment valuation as indicated by the lot's usage decision. In turn, the activities of the calibration inspection are confirmed for the maintenance order.

Q-188: A. Define inspection interval

A maintenance plan is the central planning object for a calibration inspection. Maintenance plan items control the maintenance and inspection tasks that are performed on maintenance objects. These items control when maintenance or inspection tasks are

performed using maintenance cycles for which time and performance-based inspection intervals are defined. Depending on Customizing settings, as a maintenance plan is scheduled, maintenance calls are created and converted to orders when the calls are due. As an order is released, an inspection lot is created and the maintenance task list – equipment, functional or general task list -- is selected and assigned to the maintenance plan. Each task list structure contains operations and possibly sub-operations that describe the work to be performed during a calibration inspection. Inspection characteristics that describe what will be inspected using quantitative or qualitative inspection specifications can be assigned to the task list. Following the selection and assignment of the task list, the calibration inspection operations are performed in chronological order and characteristic inspection results are recorded and valuated. Next, based on the valuation of the inspection characteristics, a usage decision for the inspection lot is documented and the inspection lot is completed. The completion of the calibration inspection triggers an update to the test equipment status in the equipment master record to reflect the test equipment valuation as indicated by the lot's usage decision. In turn, the activities of the calibration inspection are confirmed for the maintenance order.

Q–189:   A. Created at the maintenance plan level and C. Time or performance based

A maintenance plan is the central planning object for a calibration inspection. Maintenance plan items control the maintenance and inspection tasks that are

performed on maintenance objects. These items control when maintenance or inspection tasks are performed using maintenance cycles for which time and performance-based inspection intervals are defined. Depending on Customizing settings, as a maintenance plan is scheduled, maintenance calls are created and converted to orders when the calls are due. As an order is released, an inspection lot is created and the maintenance task list is selected and assigned to the maintenance plan. Each task list structure contains operations and possibly sub-operations that describe the work to be performed during a calibration inspection. Inspection characteristics that describe what will be inspected using quantitative or qualitative inspection specifications can be assigned to the task list. Following the selection and assignment of the task list, the calibration inspection operations are performed in chronological order and characteristic inspection results are recorded and valuated. Next, based on the valuation of the inspection characteristics, a usage decision for the inspection lot is documented and the inspection lot is completed. The completion of the calibration inspection triggers an update to the test equipment status in the equipment master record to reflect the test equipment valuation as indicated by the lot's usage decision. In turn, the activities of the calibration inspection are confirmed for the maintenance order.

Q-190:   B. Maintenance plan

A maintenance plan is the central planning object for a calibration inspection. Maintenance plan items control the maintenance and inspection tasks that are

performed on maintenance objects. These items control when maintenance or inspection tasks are performed using maintenance cycles for which time and performance-based inspection intervals are defined. Depending on Customizing settings, as a maintenance plan is scheduled, maintenance calls are created and converted to orders when the calls are due. As an order is released, an inspection lot is created and the maintenance task list – equipment, functional or general task list -- is selected and assigned to the maintenance plan. Each task list structure contains operations and possibly sub-operations that describe the work to be performed during a calibration inspection. Inspection characteristics that describe what will be inspected using quantitative or qualitative inspection specifications can be assigned to the task list. Following the selection and assignment of the task list, the calibration inspection operations are performed in chronological order and characteristic inspection results are recorded and valuated. Next, based on the valuation of the inspection characteristics, a usage decision for the inspection lot is documented and the inspection lot is completed. The completion of the calibration inspection triggers an update to the test equipment status in the equipment master record to reflect the test equipment valuation as indicated by the lot's usage decision. In turn, the activities of the calibration inspection are confirmed for the maintenance order.

Q-191:   A. Triggered by the maintenance plan

A maintenance plan is the central planning object for a calibration inspection. Maintenance plan items control the maintenance and inspection tasks that are

performed on maintenance objects. These items control when maintenance or inspection tasks are performed using maintenance cycles for which time and performance-based inspection intervals are defined. Depending on Customizing settings, as a maintenance plan is scheduled, maintenance calls are created and converted to orders when the calls are due. As an order is released, an inspection lot is created and the maintenance task list -- equipment, functional or general task list -- is selected and assigned to the maintenance plan. Each task list structure contains operations and possibly sub-operations that describe the work to be performed during a calibration inspection. Inspection characteristics that describe what will be inspected using quantitative or qualitative inspection specifications can be assigned to the task list. Following the selection and assignment of the task list, the calibration inspection operations are performed in chronological order and characteristic inspection results are recorded and valuated. Next, based on the valuation of the inspection characteristics, a usage decision for the inspection lot is documented and the inspection lot is completed. The completion of the calibration inspection triggers an update to the test equipment status in the equipment master record to reflect the test equipment valuation as indicated by the lot's usage decision. In turn, the activities of the calibration inspection are confirmed for the maintenance order.

Q-192: B. Activities performed to maintain maintenance objects

A maintenance plan is the central planning object for a calibration inspection. Maintenance plan items control the maintenance and inspection tasks that are performed on maintenance objects. These items control when maintenance or inspection tasks are performed using maintenance cycles for which time and performance-based inspection intervals are defined. Depending on Customizing settings, as a maintenance plan is scheduled, maintenance calls are created and converted to orders when the calls are due. As an order is released, an inspection lot is created and the maintenance task list is selected and assigned to the maintenance plan. Each task list structure contains operations and possibly sub-operations that describe the work to be performed during a calibration inspection. Inspection characteristics that describe what will be inspected using quantitative or qualitative inspection specifications can be assigned to the task list. Following the selection and assignment of the task list, the calibration inspection operations are performed in chronological order and characteristic inspection results are recorded and valuated. Next, based on the valuation of the inspection characteristics, a usage decision for the inspection lot is documented and the inspection lot is completed. The completion of the calibration inspection triggers an update to the test equipment status in the equipment master record to reflect the test equipment valuation as indicated by the lot's usage decision. In turn, the activities of the calibration inspection are confirmed for the maintenance order.

Q-193:   A. Central planning object

A maintenance plan is the central planning object for a calibration inspection. Maintenance plan items control the maintenance and inspection tasks that are performed on maintenance objects. These items control when maintenance or inspection tasks are performed using maintenance cycles for which time and performance-based inspection intervals are defined. Depending on Customizing settings, as a maintenance plan is scheduled, maintenance calls are created and converted to orders when the calls are due. As an order is released, an inspection lot is created and the maintenance task list is selected and assigned to the maintenance plan. Each task list structure contains operations and possibly sub-operations that describe the work to be performed during a calibration inspection. Inspection characteristics that describe what will be inspected using quantitative or qualitative inspection specifications can be assigned to the task list. Following the selection and assignment of the task list, the calibration inspection operations are performed in chronological order and characteristic inspection results are recorded and valuated. Next, based on the valuation of the inspection characteristics, a usage decision for the inspection lot is documented and the inspection lot is completed. The completion of the calibration inspection triggers an update to the test equipment status in the equipment master record to reflect the test equipment valuation as indicated by the lot's usage decision. In turn, the activities of the calibration inspection are confirmed for the maintenance order.

Q-194:   A. Determine the inspection lots that were inspected using a particular piece of test equipment and

B. Determine the inspection characteristics that were inspected using a particular piece of test equipment

In the event of the failure of a piece of test equipment, it's necessary to isolate the inspections that were conducted using the faulty equipment to identify and resolve any quality issues that may not have been identified during an inspection. The test equipment tracking report is used for this purpose. The report specifies inspection characteristics that were evaluated with a particular piece of test equipment. In addition, the tracking report identifies the work center at which an inspection occurred and the time period during which a particular piece of test equipment was located at the work center.

Q-195: A. Assignment of inspection type to maintenance order type

Test equipment is regularly inspected and calibrated to ensure that it adheres to predefined performance criteria is suitable for quality inspections. The results of the calibration inspection govern the release of the test equipment for subsequent use. The planning, scheduling and performance of calibration inspections require the master data, as well as the planning and processing functions of the Test Equipment Management component. In particular, the functions required to plan a calibration inspection include the creation of an equipment master record, measuring points with reference to class characteristics and a maintenance strategy. Also required are the creation of a task list, an inspection lot, master inspection characteristics and a maintenance plan. In turn,

Customizing requirements include the definition of an inspection type, inspection points, default values for the inspection type and an order type. Also required are the assignment of inspection type PM05 to the order type, materials to task list operations, objects to the maintenance plan items and master inspection characteristics to operations.

Q-196:   A. Record inspection results for measurement points of test equipment using measurement documents

A usage decision code for an inspection lot concludes an inspection and documents its outcome. On the basis of this code and its linkage to follow-up functions, the functions can be executed automatically. One such follow-up action is the creation of measurement documents to record inspection results for each inspection point that's defined for the test equipment. The critical values obtained by measurement readings are recorded in the documents and used to monitor a technical installation. The measurement documents are stored in the test equipment master record. The requirements for this functionality include the linkage of master inspection characteristics in the maintenance task list to measuring point master records by means of the class characteristics, as well as the creation of measuring point categories. Also required is the assignment of qualitative characteristics to the measuring point.

Q-197:   D. All of the above

A maintenance plan is the central planning object for a calibration inspection. Maintenance plan items control the maintenance and inspection tasks that are performed on maintenance objects. These items control when maintenance or inspection tasks are performed using maintenance cycles for which time and performance-based inspection intervals are defined. Depending on Customizing settings, as a maintenance plan is scheduled, maintenance calls are created and converted to orders when the calls are due. As an order is released, an inspection lot is created and the maintenance task list is selected and assigned to the maintenance plan. Each task list structure contains operations and possibly sub-operations that describe the work to be performed during a calibration inspection. Inspection characteristics that describe what will be inspected using quantitative or qualitative inspection specifications can be assigned to the task list. Following the selection and assignment of the task list, the calibration inspection operations are performed in chronological order and characteristic inspection results are recorded and valuated. Next, based on the valuation of the inspection characteristics, a usage decision for the inspection lot is documented and the inspection lot is completed. The completion of the calibration inspection triggers an update to the test equipment status in the equipment master record to reflect the test equipment valuation as indicated by the lot's usage decision. In turn, the activities of the calibration inspection are confirmed for the maintenance order.

Q-198:   A. Test equipment maintenance history is maintained in the equipment master record

The Plant Maintenance component is used to create an equipment master record for each piece of test equipment. This master record provides the means to manage test equipment at the client level, document the equipment's maintenance history, as well as the equipment's status, which the calibration inspection determines. The equipment master record is also used to maintain static information about the equipment, such as the equipment's acquisition value and dimensions and the date the equipment was acquired. Also in the master record are the equipment's manufacturer, the work center and plant at which the equipment is located, and the equipment's serial number and cost center. The equipment's maintenance intervals, which are either time or performance-based, are also stored in the equipment master record.

Q-199:   A. Change cycle modification factor

A usage decision code for an inspection lot documents the outcome of a calibration inspection and concludes the calibration inspection. On the basis of this code and its linkage to follow-up actions, individual functions can be performed automatically. One such follow-up function is the calculation of a quality score for the inspection lot. Other follow-up actions include using the cycle modification factor to update the inspection interval in the preventive maintenance plan and creating measurement documents for each measuring point to record inspection results. Additional follow-up actions include updating the status of a piece of equipment in the equipment master record to reflect the usage decision for the inspection and the technical completion of a maintenance order.

Q-200:   B. Assign qualitative characteristic with a
selected set to a measuring point

A usage decision code for an inspection lot concludes
an inspection and documents its outcome. On the
basis of this code and its linkage to follow-up functions,
the functions can be executed automatically. One such
follow-up action is the creation of measurement
documents to record inspection results for each
inspection point that's defined for the test equipment.
The critical values obtained by measurement readings
are recorded in the documents and used to monitor a
technical installation. The measurement documents are
stored in the test equipment master record. The
requirements for this functionality include the linkage
of master inspection characteristics in the maintenance
task list to measuring point master records by means of
the class characteristics, as well as the creation of
measuring point categories. Also required is the
assignment of qualitative characteristics to the
measuring point.

Q-201:   B. Change cycle modification factor

A usage decision code for an inspection lot documents
the outcome of a calibration inspection and concludes
the calibration inspection. On the basis of this code and
its linkage to follow-up actions, individual functions can
be performed automatically. One such follow-up
function is the calculation of a quality score for the
inspection lot. Other follow-up actions include using
the cycle modification factor to update the inspection

interval in the preventive maintenance plan and creating measurement documents for each measuring point to record inspection results. Additional follow-up actions include updating the status of a piece of equipment in the equipment master record to reflect the usage decision for the inspection and the technical completion of a maintenance order.

www.ingramcontent.com/pod-product-compliance
Lightning Source LLC
Chambersburg PA
CBHW070938050326
40689CB00014B/3247